The Future of Computer System Design: AI-Augmented Optimization

Shahi Par

Copyright © [2023]
Title: The Future of Computer System Design:
AI-Augmented Optimization
Author: Shahi Par

All rights reserved. No part of this publication may be reproduced, stored in a retrieval system, or transmitted in any form or by any means, electronic, mechanical, photocopying, recording, or otherwise, without the prior written permission of the publisher or author, except in the case of brief quotations embodied in critical reviews and certain other noncommercial uses permitted by copyright law.

This book was printed and published by [**Publisher's Shahi Par in [2023]**

ISBN:

Chapter 1: Introduction

Machine learning has achieved remarkable performance over the past decades in detecting objects, recognizing patterns, extracting relations, and predicting results. These tasks comprise the computational core of artificial intelligence (AI) applications and AI-augmented systems in diverse areas including computer vision, natural language processing, autonomous robots, and health care. Computer engineering, and especially, design of computer systems are relatively new application areas of AI. Prior to the recent rise of AI, the design process has been aided by computers that automatically transform an abstract description of a system into a specific hardware description. Yet, it has been left to the design experts to explore the enormous design space by leveraging their knowledge and experience. This chapter introduces the concept of AI-augmented design space exploration of computer systems and the challenges of machine learning for such applications.

1.1 Design of Computer Systems

Computers perform *computations*. Machines operate *automatically*. Advances in computing machinery has enabled humans to accomplish progressively more complex tasks in such a way that humans make higher-level decisions while offloading repeated subtasks to the specialized machines: the modern computer systems. Ranging from mighty supercomputers to ubiquitous embedded systems, computers have had and are having a tremendous impact on human life and society. In order to take advantage of those machines, humans first *design* and then build them.

'Design' can both refer to the product, as a noun, and to the process, as a verb [1]. Since this book specifically addresses the design of computer systems, I will use the term 'design' to refer to the process, while referring to the product as a 'computer system', or briefly as a 'system'. Matchett defines 'design' (from an engineer's perspective) as the process of 'achieving the optimum solution to the sum of the true needs of a particular set of circumstances' [2]. To achieve the optimum solution, designers often engage in systematic and chaotic thinking, employing both mechanical calculation and imaginative thought [1]. In the *computer-aided* design (CAD) methodology, designers may offload the systematic thinking and mechanical calculation to computers. This way, designers can cope with the excessively increasing complexity of the product and the design process, as well as exercising their creativity to solve problems at a higher level.

Modern electronic computer systems execute software instructions with hardware circuits such as central processing units (CPUs), graphical processing units (GPUs), tensor processing units (TPUs), application-specific integrated circuits (ASICs), field-programmable gate arrays (FPGAs), and other types of specialized processors or accelerators. The complexity of integrated circuits has continued to increase at an exponential pace, actualizing the phenomenon known as Moore's law [3, 4]. The very large-scale integration (VLSI) circuits of the 1970s integrated tens of thousands of transistors; today's system-on-chip (SoC) circuits host multiple billions of transistors [5, 6, 7, 8]. This outstanding growth of computational capabilities has been sustained in part by the progress in development of CAD software tools for computer systems. The designer abstractly describes the target computer system in the form of a *specification* of the system. Then, a CAD tool or a CAD flow (a chain of sequentially executed CAD tools) performs refinement steps from the higher level down to the detailed level of description to automatically generate an *implementation* of the input specification. Hence, the CAD flow facilitates the design of extremely complex systems; moreover, it does so by providing separation of concerns between the specification and the implementation.

Both in academia and in industry, CAD approaches (also frequently called 'electronic design automation (EDA)' approaches in industry) have evolved towards raising the level of abstraction. Advanced CAD flows typically include the steps of high-level synthesis (HLS),

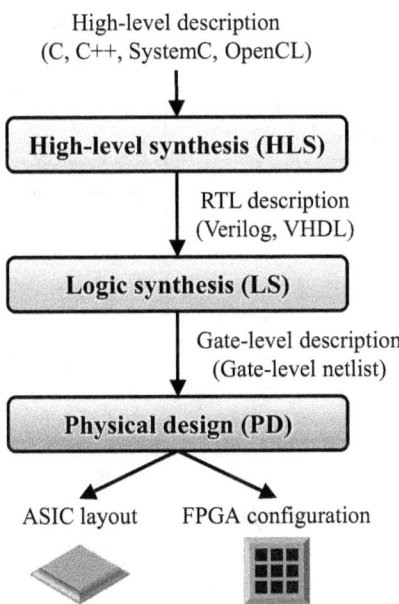

Figure 1.1: A typical computer-aided design (CAD) flow with high-level synthesis (HLS), logic synthesis (LS), and physical design (PD). Each CAD tool or tool-chain (a rounded and shaded box) transforms a higher-level specification into a lower-level implementation.

logic synthesis (LS), and physical design (PD), as shown in Fig. 1.1. An HLS tool transforms a behavioral specification (in high-level languages such as C, C++, SystemC [9], and OpenCL [10]) into a structural implementation, which describes the structures and operations of the specified system at register-transfer level (RTL) [11]. An LS tool translates an RTL specification (in hardware description languages such as Verilog [12] and VHDL [13]) into a gate-level implementation, which is a network of logic gates implementing the specified logic and functionality [14]. Given a gate-level specification (in a gate-level netlist), a PD tool or tool-chain performs placement and routing to generate a final implementation. Placement determines the location of the logic gates, and routing interconnects those gates with wires [15]. The final implementation will be a physical layout for an integrated circuit

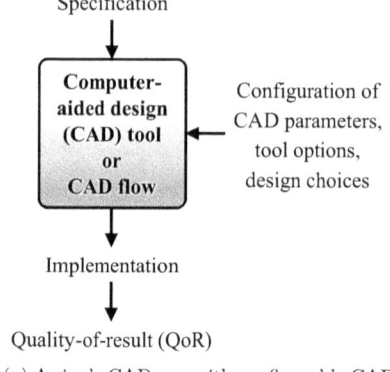 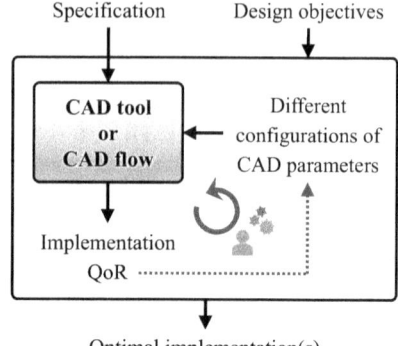

(a) A single CAD run with configurable CAD parameters. Their configuration guides the execution of CAD algorithms, which in turn affects the quality-of-result (QoR).

(b) Repeated CAD runs for a specification and design objectives in the search of optimal implementations. This process is called design space exploration (DSE).

Figure 1.2: An advanced CAD process with configurable CAD parameters.

system, and it will be a configuration bitstream for an FPGA-based system.

Most stages in CAD require the solution of many intractable (NP-hard) problems at a very large scale [16]. A single run of a CAD flow may take many hours to days, depending on the complexity of the designed system. However, a designer's task does not complete with a single run. Let us recall the aforementioned definition of design: achieving the 'optimum solution to the sum of the true needs of a particular set of circumstances'. For CAD of a particular modern electronic computer system (whose behavior is well specified), the needs are to maximize the system performance while minimizing various types of cost associated with the production and operation of the system. The principal performance (e.g., latency, throughput, accuracy) and cost (e.g., area occupation, power dissipation, wire congestion) metrics are often inversely affected by design choices [17, 18]. For instance, improving the performance by reducing the latency usually comes at the expensive cost of larger occupation of silicon area or FPGA resources. Thus, it is infeasible for CAD tools to automatically generate a final implementation that presents optimal values for all metrics of interest. Instead, advanced CAD tools and flows provide a variety of *CAD parameters* that

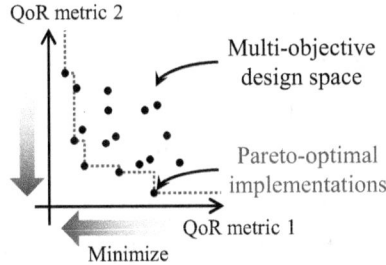
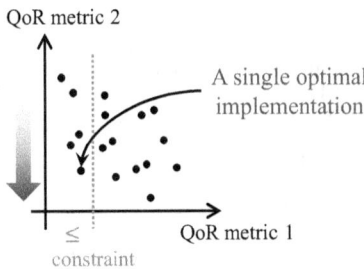
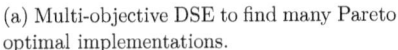

(a) Multi-objective DSE to find many Pareto optimal implementations.

(b) DSE with constraints to find a single optimal implementation.

Figure 1.3: Exploration of design spaces with multiple QoR metrics to minimize (or maximize).

affect the execution of the algorithms within the tools and, eventually, drastically impact the resulting performance and cost, also called quality-of-result (QoR), as shown in Fig. 1.2 (a). Hence, it is an essential role of designers to configure the CAD parameters in order to obtain implementations with acceptable, desirable, or optimal QoR, as shown in Fig. 1.2 (b).

1.2 Design *Space Exploration* of Computer Systems

The process of searching for the optimal CAD parameter configurations for a computer system is called *design space exploration (DSE)*. Effects of CAD parameters on QoR vary depending on the particular system being designed. Moreover, different metrics of QoR require a careful balancing of the delicate trade-offs. Therefore, designers usually test numerous configurations of different parameter values by repeatedly running the CAD tools with each configuration in order to navigate the multi-objective design space where each objective corresponds to maximizing or minimizing one QoR metric of interest. This process of DSE forms an integral part of optimizing each system, and it consumes a considerable amount of time along with computing and human resources, even with today's state-of-the-art industrial CAD flows.

Multi-objective DSE aims at minimizing or maximizing multiple, often conflicting, QoR metrics of an implementation. Fig. 1.3 (a) illustrates a design space of a specification with two QoR metrics to minimize. The black points represent distinct implementations of the same specification. For simplicity, when the objective is to minimize all metrics, one implementation is said to *Pareto dominate* another implementation if (1) the formal has QoR values less than or equal to those of the latter in all metrics, and (2) the formal has a strictly smaller QoR value than the latter for at least one metric. Among all implementations (in consideration) of a specification, an implementation that is not Pareto-dominated by any other is called *Pareto optimal* [19]. In Fig. 1.3 (a), the black points connected by the purple dotted lines correspond to the Pareto optimal implementations. A goal of the DSE process is to identify all CAD parameter configurations that lead the CAD tools to generate the Pareto optimal implementations. This is mainly for reusing the specification in various circumstances.

The intellectual property (IP) reuse methodology has become one of the keys for the productivity improvement of modern computer system design [20]. A final implementation that exhibits predetermined QoR is classified as *hard IP*, whereas a higher-level specification that can be synthesized to have various QoR is *soft IP*. A library of reusable IP blocks with various timing, area, and power configurations allows a new system integrator to reuse the IP blocks with the best configurations to meet the target system's requirements [21]. Thus, it is often the goal of DSE with HLS tools, especially for designing reusable hardware accelerators, to find many, if not all, of the CAD parameter configurations that are mapped to the Pareto optimal implementations, or to the implementations of close QoR values to those of some Pareto optimal ones [22].

LS and PD tools, on the other hand, generate highly optimized hard IP for a target system (which could be reused as well). Many stages of optimization in PD (e.g., placement, routing, post-routing optimization) are order of magnitude more computationally expensive than those in HLS. Such high complexity of the CAD problems makes it infeasible to find all Pareto optimal implementations during the DSE, especially for complex VLSI systems with stringent time-to-market requirements. Moreover, such exploration has a lower payoff when done with LS and PD than with HLS [23]. Therefore, another goal of DSE – also called *parameter tuning* or *CAD flow tuning* with respect to this goal – is to find a single optimal implementation that minimizes (or maximizes) an objective function subject to a set of constraints, as shown in Fig. 1.3 (b). The objective function is usually defined as a single QoR metric, or as a scalarization (e.g., a weighted sum) of multiple QoR metrics [24]. The constraints describe a valid range of values for certain QoR metrics. For instance, the goal with an LS process is to find an implementation 'with a minimum area while meeting the delay constraint' [25]. The ultimate goal with another LS and PD process is 'to reach timing closure at the lowest achievable power' [26].

Strategies for DSE include exhaustively evaluating every possible configuration; randomly sampling the design space; leveraging the designer's knowledge, experience, and expertise; developing analytical models for QoR estimation; and applying heuristics or meta-heuristics, such as genetic algorithms and simulated annealing [27, 22]. Since an exhaustive search is impracticable, it is crucial to discover the optimal, or near optimal, configurations after running the CAD tools or flows as few times as possible. Recently, the proliferation of AI and machine learning in a wide variety of application areas has motivated the advent of AI-augmented DSE of computer systems [22, 28].

1.3 *AI-Augmented* Design Space Exploration of Computer Systems

AI is 'the science and engineering of making intelligent machines' which have 'computational ... ability to achieve goals in the world' [29]. Since Turing proposed in 1950 to consider the question 'Can machines think?' [30], researchers have attempted to 'find how to make machines use language, form abstractions and concepts, solve kinds of problems now [or, then] reserved for humans, and improve themselves' [31]. While the rate of progress in AI thereafter has been 'unpredictable', twenty-first century AI has seen extraordinary advances fueled by 'the maturing of machine learning' [32]. Such maturation has been supported by the availability of large-scale data (also called 'Big Data'), and the capabilities of modern high-performance computer systems [32, 33, 34]. Consequently, AI has been deployed or integrated in a variety of AI-assisted, AI-based, AI-centric, AI-driven, AI-enabled, and AI-powered applications in diverse domains [35, 36, 37, 38, 39, 40].

Design of optimal computer systems is another goal that could be targeted by AI, but not solely by AI – as of today and in the near future. A more thorough definition of 'design' is derived in a survey by Evbuomwan et al. (from mechanical engineers' perspective):

> [Design is] The process of establishing requirements based on human needs, transforming them into performance specification and functions, which are then mapped and converted (subject to constraints) into design solutions (using creativity, scientific principles and technical knowledge) that can be economically manufactured and produced [41].

Design of computer systems involves (1) establishing requirements, (2) transforming them into a specification, and (3) converting them into implementations that are optimal or feasible. The first two steps are led by humans. 'The current state of AI technology is still far short of the field's founding aspiration of recreating full human-like intelligence in machines,' states the *2021 book Panel* of the long-term investigation of AI, *One Hundred Year book on AI* [42]. It is not only the limited capabilities of the current AI, but more importantly, the impact and responsibility of the decisions made in the first two steps that require those decisions to be made or confirmed by humans. The third step, which is the main focus of this **book**, has been led by humans, aided by computers. AI may assist them.

Initially, human designers manually produced the physical layout. Development and sophistication of the CAD tools enabled designers to put more effort into producing the specification and performing DSE while offloading to CAD tools the repeated subtask of converting the specification into implementations. These activities, by both the designers and CAD tools, demand *intelligence*, namely creativity, scientific principles, and technical knowledge (as noted by Evbuomwan et al.). The goal of AI-augmented design or DSE is to develop an AI system with such *intelligence* to boost both design productivity and quality. Many approaches have been proposed over the past decade targeting various stages of CAD [28]. More recently, Google and Nvidia have released that their next-generation computer systems are designed by AI-driven systems, while Synopsys and Cadence have announced AI-based optimization platforms targeting their CAD tool products [43]. At the core of all those AI applications for computer system design is machine learning[1].

1.4 *Machine Learning for* AI-Augmented Design Space Exploration of Computer Systems

Machine learning is 'a subfield of AI' that addresses the question of '*how to build computers that improve automatically through experience*' [34, 44]. A subcategory of machine learning that has been extensively studied is supervised learning, where machines use a labeled set of data, i.e., tuples of (input data; output label), in order to predict the output label from the unseen input data. For classification problems, the labels are classes or categories. For instance, in the problem of handwritten digit recognition, the goal is to learn a model that takes in an image consisting of pixel values and outputs the corresponding digit: $0, 1, \cdots, 9$ [45]. This model is trained using a labeled set of (input: image; output: digit) data. For regression problems, the labels are continuous values, such as the temperature, house prices, or the amount of carbon dioxide emissions. During DSE of a computer system, designers run CAD tools a large number of times with various CAD parameter or flow configurations to learn the corresponding QoR. This DSE problem can be translated into a regression problem with (input: specification, CAD configuration; output: QoR).

Multiple challenges arise in this problem due to the characteristics of CAD problems.

1. Many machine learning applications utilize data obtained from huge collections of users' input and public databases for a single problem. The QoR-prediction problem for each system suffers from limited availability of data obtained from expensive CAD runs.

---
[1]Not all, although a majority, of AI applications involve machine learning.

Especially, an industrial CAD flow specifies hundreds of separate CAD parameters, resulting in an extreme curse of dimensionality. Hence, I propose to learn from the experience (labeled datasets) not only with the target computer system, but also with *other* systems.

2. Different systems exhibit different configuration-QoR relationship. As a result, a model learned from a few previously explored systems cannot be directly exploited to predict the QoR for new target systems. Hence, I propose to learn from the experience with *many* other systems. Then, in order to successfully learn from many other heterogeneous systems, it is required to identify each system's characteristics and its relationship with other systems.

3. Designers apply unique sets of CAD configurations during the DSE of each individual system. This makes it harder to learn from previous DSE results. Especially in HLS, the specification heterogeneity leads to broad CAD configuration heterogeneity across specifications. Hence, I propose to collaborate with designers, augmenting their performance with AI, and to transfer common knowledge across the design tasks.

To address the above challenges and improve the performance of AI-augmented DSE, I propose to flexibly connect the elements of the many QoR-prediction problems with one another. My **book** is that *The exploration of the design space of a computer system can be effectively augmented by artificial intelligence via learning from the experience with the design and optimization of other systems.*

For the design of industrial high-performance processors, I propose a novel collaborative recommender system approach that learns hidden features from the interactions (CAD runs) of many *users* (computer systems) and *items* (configuration of design parameters). To cope with the curse of dimensionality, the item features are decomposed into features of item attributes (individual parameters). The combined model predicts QoR for each user-item pair.

For the design of application-specific accelerators, I present a series of neural network models in the order of evolution towards the proposed mixed-sharing *transfer learning* model. Transfer learning aims at leveraging knowledge gained from previous problems; however, due to the target computer system and design parameter heterogeneities, the model needs to distinguish which piece of that knowledge should be transferred.

The proposed machine learning approaches aim to not only use experiential knowledge as designers do but also to ultimately assist designers by providing alternative insights and suggesting optimization possibilities for new systems. As an effort in this direction, I develop an AI-augmented DSE tool that exploits the aforementioned models and *generates* recommended CAD configurations for new target systems.

1.5 Contributions and Outline

My research contributions span across HLS, LS, and PD stages of CAD (shown in Fig. 1.1) and address DSE problems of both searching for Pareto-optimal implementations (Fig. 1.3(a)) and searching for a single optimal implementation (Fig. 1.3(b)). The contributions are summarized as follows:

- A recommender system approach for industrial LS and PD flows [46, 47]

- A transfer learning approach for HLS flows [48] (Best Paper Award)

- A classification of machine-learning-based approaches for design optimization ([49], a book chapter under submission, and a survey paper in preparation)

- AI-augmented DSE by learning from the experience with other computer systems, configuration spaces, technology, and CAD tools (All of the above work, and a **book** article in preparation)

The rest of this **book** is organized as follows. **Chapter 2** presents a typical design process of a modern computer system, as a background for the research problems addressed in this book. **Chapter 3** proposes a collaborative recommender system approach for AI-augmented DSE with LS and PD flows for industrial high-performance processors. **Chapter 4** proposes a transfer learning approach for AI-augmented DSE with HLS flows for specialized accelerators. **Chapter 5** reviews and categorizes machine-learning-based approaches for DSE with CAD of computer systems. **Chapter 6** presents the future work and concluding remarks.

Chapter 2: Background

A monolithic integrated circuit, also called an integrated circuit, a microelectronic circuit, a microchip, or a chip, is a complete circuit or set of circuits manufactured on a single piece of semiconductor material [50]. Its miniaturizability and scalability have brought about the impressive success of the microelectronic industry since the 1960s. Today, it serves as the essential component of most of the contemporary computers, ranging from supercomputers and cloud servers to embedded systems and IoT (Internet-of-things) devices. Design of such computer systems has been facilitated and expedited by CAD methodology, which has evolved in the direction of raising the level of abstraction. The first PD tools date back to the 1960s, LS tools to the 1980s, and HLS tools to the 1990s [15, 51]. This chapter first provides a brief historical perspective on the emergence of integrated circuits. Then, it introduces the major stages of modern CAD flows in the reverse order of their development, following the order of their execution in today's CAD flows.

2.1 Emergence of Integrated Circuits: A Historical Perspective

Going back in history, Turing proposed in 1936 a mathematical model of computing machines that laid the foundation of modern computers [52]. The first electronic calculating machine was built by Atanasoff and Berry in 1939, using a *vacuum tube* (which controls the flow of electrons in a vacuum) as a *switch* or amplifier to control the flow of electric current [53, 54]. *ENIAC* (Electronic Numerical Integrator and Computer), the first general-purpose electronic computing machine was built during the Second World War and presented to the public in 1946 [55]. It was the fastest and *large-scale* at the time, while being equipped with about 17,000 vacuum tubes, weighing 26 tons, occupying 440 cubic meters, and consuming

174 kilowatts of electricity – not a scalable technology [54].

Smaller and less power-consuming switches to control electronic signals, called *transistors*, were created by the Bell Labs scientists, Shockley, Bardeen, and Brattain in 1947 [56]. Transistors are made from *semiconductor* materials, such as silicon and germanium. *Semiconductors* have electrical properties that are between conductors and insulators, and their conductivity can be controlled by *doping*, i.e., adding impurities. The first transistors were made from germanium; later, silicon has become the dominant material, as it offers advantages of higher operating temperatures, breakdown voltage, and power-handling ability [54]. The race for *miniaturization* of electronic circuits intensified until 1958, when Kilby at Texas Instruments invented and demonstrated the first (hybrid) *integrated circuits*, with on-chip components connected by external wires [57, 58]. After a half year, Noyce at Fairchild Semiconductor independently invented the first *monolithic* integrated circuits, with all wires and components on a single chip [59, 60]. The inventions of transistors and integrated circuits have revolutionized the electronics industry and were recognized by the Nobel Prize in Physics in 1956 and 2000, respectively [61, 62].

Integrated circuits consist of different components, such as transistors, resistors, capacitors, and diodes, that are all made from the same materials (usually silicon) for integration [58, 54]. Those circuit components can be analogous to the parts of speech, such as nouns, verbs, adjectives, and adverb, as noted by Reid [63]. Each component has its own function, and by connecting them in different ways, we can obtain the sentences or circuits that perform in different ways [54]. It is the designers' task to connect those components to build a circuit that performs as desired. At first, designers produced by hand a geometric description of circuits, called a layout, on papers and films (for fabricating integrated circuits on semiconductor substrates by photolithography) [64].

Technology continued to advance to allow integrated circuits to incorporate thousands of transistors on a single chip by the late 1960s. The computers built with those integrated circuits were harnessed to speed the development process and eliminate errors in the design of the next generation of integrated circuits [65]. IBM and Fairchild developed in-house graphical CAD tools for circuit layout design and simulation [66, 67, 68, 69]. Their work, along with the academic project SPICE (Simulation Program with Integrated Circuit Emphasis) laid the foundation for CAD of integrated circuits [67, 70, 71].

2.2 Computer-Aided Design for Modern Computer Systems

Design methodology for integrated circuits has advanced to achieve increasing levels of automation and abstraction. The automation of computation has allowed designers to offload the fixed computational subtasks to computers, while solving problems that require higher degree of creativity. The abstraction level refers to the level at which designers specify circuits. By raising this level, CAD tools provide separation of concerns between the higher-level structure, behavior, or functionality, and the lower-level implementation details [72]. Such advances in CAD have supported the development of the state-of-the-art computer systems that offer high performance, energy efficiency, acceleration, and specialization.

Modern computer systems contain computational subsystems that range from general-purpose to specialized systems. Since their invention, transistors have reduced in size exponentially, resulting in an exponential increase of transistor density on a chip (Moore's law), yet still capable of maintaining constant power density (Dennard scaling) [3, 4, 73]. Thanks to the VLSI technology and advanced CAD, today's high-performance processors and systems-on-chip include multiple billions of transistors on a single chip [5, 6, 7, 8]. Most of them include general-purpose processors that can run an extensive variety of applications. The technology scaling, however, has slowed down due to the physical limitations and the end of Dennard scaling around 2005 [74]. In order to improve the performance while maintaining the power dissipation and heat generation below thresholds, multi-core and heterogeneous architectures have emerged. State-of-the-art SoC architectures may include multiple and heterogeneous subsystems such as general-purpose processors, special-purpose processors (e.g., GPUs, TPUs, digital signal processors, and neural processors), and application-specific hardware accelerators [75]. The specialized processors or accelerators execute the specific instructions or applications that they are designed for. Programmable logic devices (e.g., FPGAs) and coarse-grain reconfigurable devices (e.g., coarse-grain reconfigurable arrays) can be configured after fabrication to execute (a group of) specific functionalities. They can be configured to implement specialized processors or accelerators, and reconfigured for different applications [76, 77, 78, 79].

A *computer system* in this **book** refers to a computational subsystem, be it general-purpose, specialized, or reconfigurable, that is often designed (or configured) independently from one another. By extension, the term also refers to a full computer system that in-cludes those subsystems. Ch. 3 addresses the design of high-performance general-purpose processors, and Ch. 4 focuses on the design of various specialized accelerators. The following subsections depict an exemplary CAD flow for modern, electronic, digital[1], and synchronous[2] computer systems, which belong to the dominant type of modern computer systems.

2.2.1 High-Level Synthesis

A typical CAD flow for a computer system today includes HLS, LS, and PD. To take a closer look at the design process, let us recall the definition of 'design' by Evbuomwan et al. from the previous chapter. Design is the process of

(i) establishing requirements based on human needs,

(ii) transforming them into performance specification and functions,

(iii) mapping and converting them (subject to constraints) into design solutions (using creativity, scientific principles and technical knowledge) that can be economically manufactured and produced [41].

---

[1]Digital circuits deal with discrete levels of signals: e.g., a high voltage representing '1' and a low voltage representing '0' in binary systems. Analog circuits, on the contrary, deal with continuous signal values.

[2]In a synchronous digital circuit, an oscillating clock signal determines when the state of memory elements is changed (values written or read): e.g., on the rising clock edge. Asynchronous circuits do not have global clock.

Let us assume that (i) a designer, Danny, was asked to design a low-power real-time accelerator for a specific artificial neural network (ANN) application (*human needs*). Danny determines the algorithm, function, or behavior of the ANN application, and confirms system requirements such as power and latency (*requirements*). Then, (ii) Danny generates a specification from the requirements determined in the previous step. The algorithm, function, or behavior of the application is transformed into a high-level specification written in a high-level language, e.g., C, C++, SystemC [9], or OpenCL [10] (*function specification*). The system requirements are quantified, e.g., target or maximum values of the power and latency are set (*performance specification*). Those values are sometimes given by the customer or determined from a larger design project. After generating the specification, (iii) Danny runs an HLS tool to convert it into RTL implementations (*map and convert into design solutions*). The HLS tool uses the synthesis algorithms (*scientific principles*) and an RTL component library (*technical knowledge*). Aided by the HLS tool, Danny performs DSE to minimize the power, latency (*performance specification*), and resource utilization (*economically manufactured and produced*).

Fig. 2.1 illustrates an overview of a typical HLS process. The HLS tool takes in a high-level specification and generates an RTL implementation of it [11]. The tool may refer to high-level libraries (which the designer used in the specification) for front-end compilation. The RTL component library provides information required in the generation of RTL implementations that consist of those components. The designer can constrain, guide, and control the HLS process with *design parameters* as shown on the right in Fig. 2.1.

Compilation

First, the high-level specification is compiled into a formal model of computation. A model of a system is a representation that shows relevant features without associated details, and formal models have a well-defined syntax and semantics for interpretation and transformation [14]. A formal model in HLS generally exhibits the data and control depen-

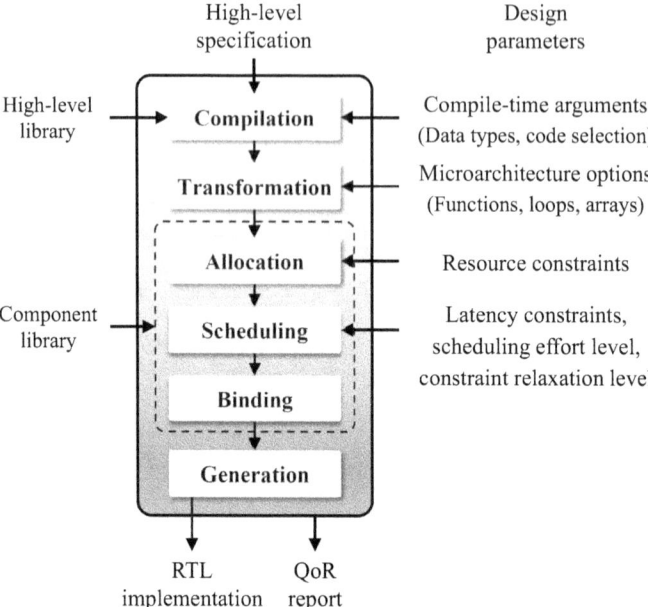

Figure 2.1: A typical design process with an HLS tool that translates a high-level specification into an RTL implementation as guided by the design parameters.

dencies between the operations without language-dependent details.

Let us take our designer Danny's ANN accelerator as an example. ANNs usually consist of interconnected layers of nodes, where each node contains a value and each layer can be represented as a vector (or a tensor of a higher dimension). Starting from a given input layer, the next layer is often computed by performing matrix multiplications to the previous layer, adding a bias, and applying a non-linear activation function. This part can be expressed as follows:

$$y = f(A \cdot x + b), \tag{2.1}$$

where x and y represent the previous and the next layer, respectively; and A is the weight matrix, b is the bias vector, and f is the activation function (e.g., *tanh*, *sigmoid*, a rectified linear unit, or *softmax*) for computing the next layer.

```c
void add_bias(dType b[n_next], dType y[n_next]) {
    int i;
    for (i = 0; i < n_next; i++)
        y[i] = y[i] + b[i];
}

void apply_tanh(dType y[n_next]) {
    int i;
    for (i = 0; i < n_next; i++)
        y[i] = tanh(y[i]);
}

void process_layer(dType x[n_pre], dType A[n_next][n_pre],
    dType b[n_next], dType y[n_next]) {
    int i,j;
    dType temp;
    for (i = 0; i < n_next; i++) {
        temp = (dType) 0.0;
        for(j = 0; j < n_pre; j++)
            temp = temp + A[i][j] * x[j];
        y[i] = temp;
    }
    add_bias(b, y);
    apply_tanh(y);
}
```

Listing 2.1: A high-level specification in C. The top function (to become the top level of the implementation) is `process_layer` which computes Eq. 2.1.

```
1    r0 = 0                  // i = 0
2
3    Block_1:
4    r1 = 0                  // j = 0
5    r5 = 0                  // sum = 0
6    r9 = r3 + r0 * n_pre    // address of A[i]
7
8    Block_2:
9    r6 = load(r9 + r1)      // load A[i][j]
10   r7 = load(r2 + r1)      // load x[j]
11   r8 = r6 * r7            // temp = A[i][j] * x[j]
12   r5 = r5 + r8            // sum = sum + temp
13   r1 = r1 + 1             // j++
14   eval r1 != n_pre        // ctrl = (j != n_pre)
15   cjump Block_2           // jump to Block_2 if ctrl is True
16
17   Block_3:
18   store(r4 + r0, r5)      // store y[i]
19   r0 = r0 + 1             // i++
20   eval r0 != n_next       // ctrl2 = (i != n_next)
21   cjump Block_1           // jump to Block_1 if ctrl2 is True
22
23   Block_4:
24   call add_bias, r10, r4  // subfunction add_bias
25   call apply_tanh, r4     // subfunction apply_tanh
```

Listing 2.2: An intermediate representation of the body of `process_layer` from Listing 2.1.

Given the above requirements, Danny produces a specification in C as shown in Listing 2.1. Function `process_layer` computes Eq. 2.1, where `n_pre` denotes the number of nodes in the previous layer x, and `n_next` is for the next layer y. `dType` is a user defined data type whose definition is in a header file or in a high-level library. Danny defines it as a native C type, such as `float`, for the software version, and selects a fixed-point data type for HLS. Function `tanh` shown in line 10 is also provided by a high-level library.

The compilation process involves preprocessing, lexical analysis, parsing, and semantic analysis. After compilation, a formal model of the specification, called *intermediate representation*, can be obtained as shown in Listing 2.2[3]. This can be further translated into a *control and data flow graph*, which is another formal model of the specification as follows. The intermediate representation is partitioned into basic blocks, which allow only sequential execution of instructions except the entry and exit points. A control flow graph is a directed graph whose nodes represent the basic blocks and directed edges represent the control flow between the blocks. Fig. 2.2 (a) shows a control flow graph of the body of `process_layer` from Listing 2.2. The computation in each node (block) of the control flow graph can be represented by a data flow graph. A data flow graph is a directed graph whose nodes represent the operations (e.g., `Ld` (load), ×, +, and ≠) and directed edges represent the data dependency. Fig. 2.2 (b) illustrates a data flow graph of *Block* 2 in `process_layer`. The left subgraph corresponds to lines 10 – 13 of the intermediate representation in Listing 2.2, which compute the sum of products of elements from the weight matrix A and from the previous layer vector x. The right subgraph represents lines 14 – 15, which update the index j and compute a control signal *ctrl* as a result of `eval` in line 15. This signal *ctrl* is used to control the flow that goes out of *Block* 2, as shown in Fig. 2.2 (a). A combination of a control flow graph and a data flow graph for each block in the control flow graph is called a *control and data flow graph*. Since the basic blocks allow only sequential execution, the data flow graph for each block is acyclic by construction. Some HLS tools enforce that all data

---

[3]An *intermediate representation* is a representation of a software program between the source code and the machine code. A software compiler usually produces this as an internal representation.

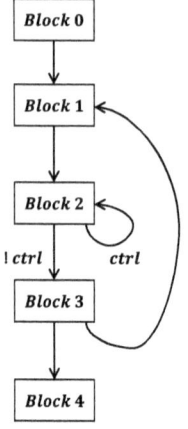 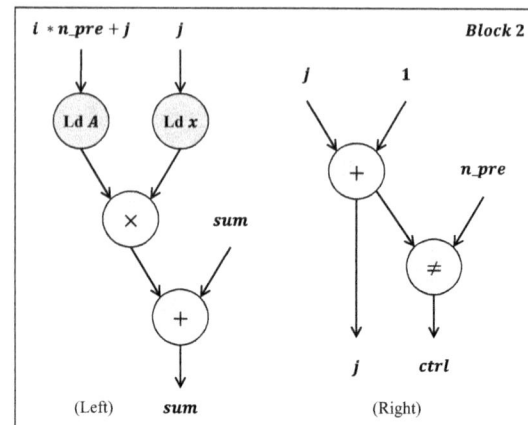

(a) A control flow graph of process_layer. Block 2's computation is presented in (b).

(b) A data flow graph of Block 2 in process_layer. The left and right subgraphs correspond to lines 10 – 13 and lines 14 – 15 of the intermediate representation in Listing 2.2, respectively.

Figure 2.2: A control and data flow graph of the body of process_layer from Listing 2.2.

flow graphs remain acyclic throughout the synthesis process.

Design parameters for the compilation process include compile-time arguments such as data type definitions (e.g., dType), code selection (e.g., an alternative version of the same functionality), library selection, parallelism options (e.g., number of parallel threads), and compiler optimizations (e.g., -O0 or -O3).

Transformation

In addition to the front-end compiler optimizations, the formal model (e.g., an intermediate representation or a control and data flow graph) may undergo a set of semantic-preserving transformations. In some cases, those transformations are automated; in others, they are guided by the designer [14]. Design parameters applied during this process determine microarchitectural details of the implementation. The major transformation parameters are listed below in three categories. State-of-the-art commercial HLS tools support most (but not necessarily all) of them, possibly with different names [80, 81, 82]. Some parameters become effective when certain conditions related to the target transformation are satisfied.

- Function transformations: `function_inline`, `function_instantiate`, `convert_to_lookup`.

    Danny's top function `process_layer` contains two subfunction calls, `add_bias` and `apply_tanh`. If those function calls are *inlined*, they dissolve into the calling function, `process_layer`, and may share components in the RTL implementation. Otherwise, the callee functions are *instantiated*; they remain as separate hierarchy blocks in the RTL, and do not share components with the upper level blocks.

    A possible benefit of `function_inline` is that the scope of application of some optimization techniques is enlarged [14]. However, if the same function is called multiple times, inlining them every time may result in the increased area or resource utilization. In that case, `function_instantiate` will instead have a single block of implementation used multiple times, as long as the function calls are at the same level of hierarchy.

    `convert_to_lookup` converts a combinational function call into a table lookup. Inputs to the function drive the address of the table (array) element, and the values read out of the table drive the outputs of the function. This conversion may be useful for combinational functions with long latency, as it can improve the timing [81].

- Loop transformations: `loop_break`, `loop_unroll`, `loop_pipeline`, `loop_flatten`, `loop_merge`.

    Fig. 2.3 illustrates the effect of four loop transformations on time and resource. `loop_break` inserts states so that each iteration of the loop takes at least one clock cycle, and the iterations are executed in a sequence [81] (Fig. 2.3 (a)). `loop_unroll` replaces the loop by as many instances of its body as the number of loop iterations, allowing some or all of the iterations to occur in parallel (if data dependencies and resources allow) [14, 80] (Fig. 2.3 (b)). *Complete* unrolling can be applied only when the loop has a data-independent exit conditions [14]. For this, Danny has to explicitly assign or define values to n_pre and n_next. When those values are not determined at design time, Danny can use upper bound values to state the loop exit conditions, and execute the loop body only when the iteration counter value is less than n_pre or n_next at runtime. *Partial* unrolling creates as many copies of the loop body as the given unrolling factor. For instance, Fig. 2.3 (c) shows the partial unrolling of the loop in Fig. 2.3 (a) by a factor of 2. loop_pipeline allows the overlapped execution of loop bodies, as shown in Fig. 2.3 (d). When pipelining loops, the designer may specify the initiation interval, the minimum latency interval, and the maximum latency interval. The initiation interval (denoted by the pink arrow in the figure) is the number of clock cycles between two consecutive executions of the loop body. Due to loop-carried dependencies, the problem of finding the minimum initiation interval of a given loop is known to be NP-complete [83]. Thus, commercial HLS tools often require the designer to specify this interval when applying loop pipelining [84, 81, 80]. The latency interval (the blue arrow) refers to the number of clock cycles to complete the execution of a single loop body instance. As shown in Fig. 2.3, loop_break may be used to minimize the area, loop_unroll to reduce the latency and increase the throughput, and loop_pipeline to optimize altogether the throughput, resource utilization, and the number of concurrent memory accesses.

loop_flatten removes the loop hierarchy by flattening the innermost loop into a single outer loop, when only the innermost loop contains loop-body contents. In the RTL implementation, it requires one clock cycle to move from an outer loop to an inner loop, and from an inner loop to an outer loop; hence, flattening nested loops may save clock cycles and allow them to be optimized as a single loop [80]. loop_merge combines consecutive loops at the same level of hierarchy into a single loop. The loop bounds of all merged loops must be a constant or a variable of the same value. This transformation may reduce the overall latency (in RTL for transitioning between

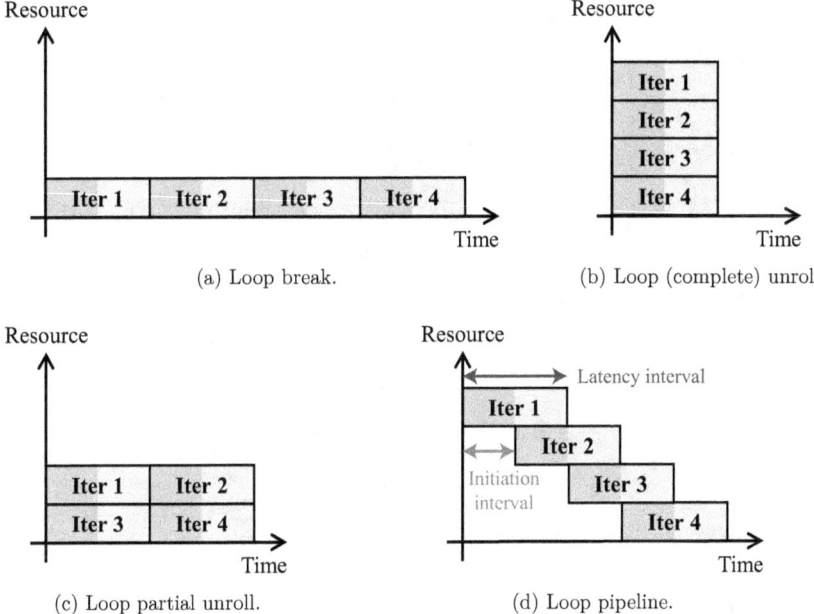

Figure 2.3: Effect of loop transformations in HLS.

merged loops), increase sharing of components among the loops, and improve logic optimization [80].

- Array transformations: `array_flatten`, `allocate_memory`, `array_merge`, `array_split`, `array_restructure`.

Some arrays in the specification are built into memories, either as a set of flat registers, with a built-in memory, with a prototype memory (as a placeholder), or with a vendor memory from the component library. `array_flatten` transforms the array into a set of registers, replacing all read and write operations to the array with equivalent reading and writing of the variables that each represent an element of the array [81]. This transformation may reduce the area and latency when the flattened arrays are small and heavily used. `allocate_memory` creates the specified type and implementation of memory (e.g., built-in memory, random access memory (RAM), block RAM (BRAM), ultra RAM (URAM), or read-only memory (ROM)) and binds it to the array. The numbers of read, write, and read/write ports of the memory indicate how many read and write operations can be performed in parallel at the same clock cycle.

`array_merge` combines multiple arrays into a single array, which may be smaller than multiple individual arrays. `array_split`, on the other hand, splits a single array into multiple smaller arrays. The split method can be specified among cyclic, block, and complete [80]. This transformation may improve the memory access parallelism at the cost of an increased area. `array_restructure` changes the number of elements (words) in an array. The array can be scaled up (increased number of words with decreased data width) or scaled down (decreased number of words with increased data width) in multiples of powers of 2 [81].

Allocation

From the formal model after the transformations, the data dependency part (also represented as a data flow graphs) is translated into a datapath, while the control dependency part (also represented as a control flow graph) becomes a finite state machine that controls the datapath. The datapath is generated through the steps of allocation, scheduling, and binding, which may occur concurrently or in various orders.

Allocation determines the type and quantity of hardware resources (e.g., functional units, storage units, and interconnection units) to be used in the implementation [85, 86]. The *functional* units (e.g., arithmetic logic units, multipliers, shifters, and other custom units) implement operations. The *storage* units (e.g., registers, register files, and memories) implement variables and arrays. The *interconnection* units (e.g., multiplexers and buses) connect the storage and functional components to transfer the signals [86]. Some resources may be added during scheduling or binding. Most hardware components are selected from the RTL component library, which also provides the characteristics, such as area, timing, and power,

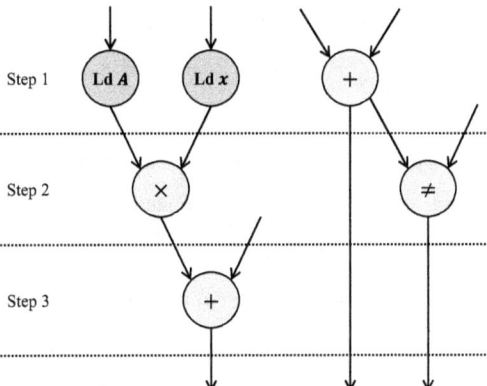

Figure 2.4: An example of scheduling of the data flow graph from Fig. 2.2 (b). The dotted lines represent discrete time steps. In this example, each operation is assumed to take a single time step.

of each component.

Resource constraints specify the maximum number of hardware resources, operations, functions, or IP cores. This may reduce the utilization of the specified resources, possibly reducing the area and increasing the latency.

Scheduling

Scheduling maps a set of operations in the formal model onto a set of discrete time steps (i.e., clock cycles) such that all data dependency constraints specified in the model are satisfied [23]. Fig. 2.4 shows an example of scheduling for the data flow graph in Fig. 2.2 (b). It is assumed that each operation in this example takes a single time step, but some functional units that implement certain operations may have longer latency. Additional constraints such as resource constraints, *latency constraints*, and the *length of a clock period* are also taken into account.

The main objectives of scheduling are to minimize the total number of time steps (i.e., overall latency), and to minimize the area or resource utilization. Area is a critical QoR for integrated circuits (such as ASICs), and resource utilization is important for reconfigurable devices such as FPGAs. The scheduler exploits the component library (and the allocation results) to obtain the latency and area information of the components.

Two fundamental categories of scheduling approaches are time-constrained scheduling (to minimize the number of components) and resource-constrained scheduling (to minimize the overall latency) [85]. Since most HLS scheduling problems are NP-hard, schedulers often employ heuristic methods. Resource-constrained approaches include list-based scheduling [87] and static list scheduling, such as ASAP (as soon as possible) and ALAP (as late as possible) [88]. Time-constrained scheduling approaches include force-directed scheduling [89] and iterative refinement methods [90]. Other heuristic methods such as simulated annealing [91] and path-based scheduling [92] have been applied as well. Linear programming and integer linear programming methods formally formulate the scheduling problem [93], such as using a system of difference constraints [94]. For complex industrial scale designs, the solution space is too large and, therefore, a slack-based scheduling approach computes the sequential slack of each operation from the data flow graph and applies heuristic scheduling and binding by slack budgeting [95].

Design parameters applied during scheduling (and allocation) include resource constraints, latency constraints, the scheduling effort level, and the constraint relaxation levels. When the scheduler cannot find a feasible solution after the initial exploration (e.g., in a time limit), the scheduler employs a more time-consuming and compute-intensive method with a *high scheduling effort*, and relax some designer-specified constraints when *constraint relaxation is allowed*. Otherwise, it may notify the designer a schedule failure [81].

Binding

Binding maps each operation, variable, and interconnection in the scheduled model to a functional unit, storage unit, and interconnection unit, respectively, while maximizing resource sharing [86]. Fig. 2.5 illustrates an example of binding of the data flow graph scheduled in Fig. 2.4. The operation × is bound to a functional unit MULT. The two +

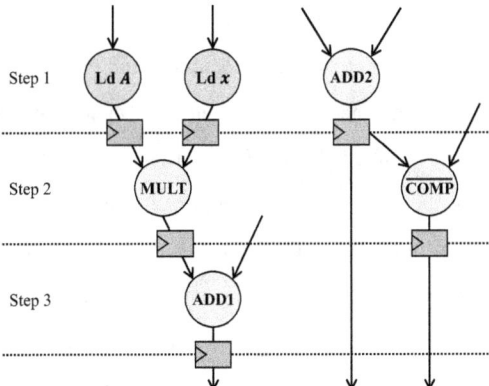

Figure 2.5: An example of binding of the data flow graph scheduled in Fig. 2.4. The operations are bound to functional units. Some variables are bound to registers, shown as the oranges boxes.

operations are bound to ADD1 (for fixed-point addition) and ADD2 (for integer addition), respectively. The operation ≠ is bound to a negated equality-comparator unit $\overline{\text{COMP}}$. Multiple operations of the same type can be bound to a common functional unit if those operations are scheduled at different time steps. Each variable that carries values across the time steps is bound to a storage unit, such as a register. In Fig. 2.5, the orange boxes on the edges crossing a time step line represent the registers. Registers can also be shared among multiple variables with mutually exclusive lifetimes. Each transfer from component to component is bound to a interconnection unit, such as a bus or a multiplexer [86]. Due to the tight relationship among the problems, binding may occur concurrently or interleaved with scheduling and allocation [14, 86, 96, 97, 98].

Generation

After allocation, scheduling, and binding, the decisions made in those steps are applied to generate an RTL description of the model written in a hardware description language (HDL) such as Verilog [12] or VHDL [13]. The RTL implementation contains the synthesized data path (consisting of the bound functional, storage, and interconnection components) and the associated controller. The controller implements the control finite state machine, by typically using registers to store the current state and combinational logic to compute the next state based on the current state and the conditions coming from the data path [99]. Some parts of the data path may be left unbound after HLS; in this case, they are bound and optimized in the LS and PD stages, using more accurate and practical timing estimates [86].

After the HLS tool generates an RTL implementation, or many implementations using different configurations of the design parameters, one last subtask remains before the designer moves onto the LS stage: *validation*. Although the implementations generated by HLS tools should be functionally equivalent to the input specification by construction, it is important to perform validation to ensure that the implementation will function correctly and to eliminate any possible design errors [14]. This is especially critical in industrial design processes, where a large volume of expensive chips are manufactured from a single implementation. Validation can be performed by *simulation* and *verification* methods [100]. Since it is not the main focus of this **book**, let us assume that Danny completes validation and starts the LS process.

2.2.2 Logic Synthesis

Fig. 2.6 illustrates a typical design process with LS. An LS tool takes in an RTL specification, either auto-generated from an HLS tool or provided by the designer, and transforms it into a gate-level implementation.

- Translation: The RTL specification (in a hardware description language such as Verilog or VHLD) is first translated into a technology-independent logic representation, such as finite state machines (for sequential components), Boolean functions (for combinational components), or logic networks (for mixed sequential and combinational components) [14].

For example, the negated equality-comparator unit $\overline{COMP}$ in Fig. 2.5 takes in two inputs, namely L and R, and outputs $f = 0$ if $L = R$, and $f = 1$ if $L \neq R$. Assuming that each of U and V represents an unsigned binary number of 8 bits, the component $\overline{COMP}$ can

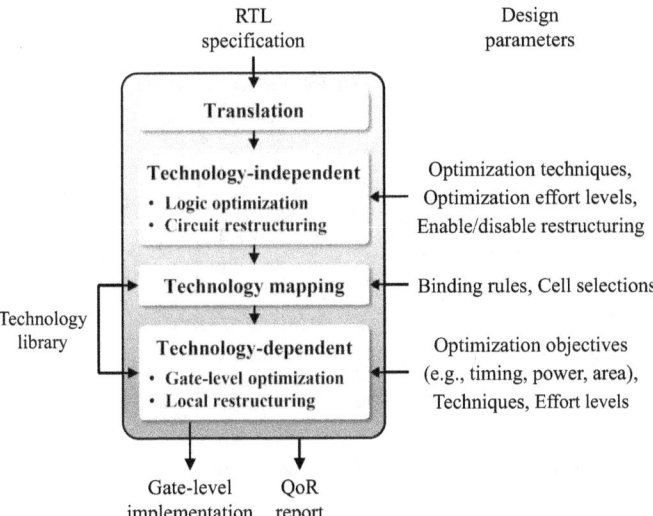

Figure 2.6: A typical design process with an LS tool that translates an RTL specification into a gate-level implementation as guided by the design parameters.

be translated into a logic network that computes f as shown in Fig 2.7. L_n and R_n denote the bit value at index n ($0 \leq n \leq 7$) of L and R, respectively. The XNOR gates at the first level determine whether a pair of bits at the same index of L and R are the same. The AND gate at the second level outputs 1 if all pairs match, and 0 otherwise. The NOT gate at the third level negates the output from the AND gate. Hence, the full network represents $\overline{\text{COMP}}$.

- Technology-independent optimization: The abstract logic representation is optimized with an objective of minimizing the complexity, e.g., in terms of the number of Karnaugh map implicants, logic gates, levels in logic networks, or states in finite state machines. The optimization methods have been investigated heavily over multiple decades for two-level combinational logic [101, 102, 103, 104], multi-level combinational logic [105, 106, 107], and sequential logic components [108, 109, 110, 111, 14]. As many of them are heuristic and iterative methods, advanced LS tools allow the

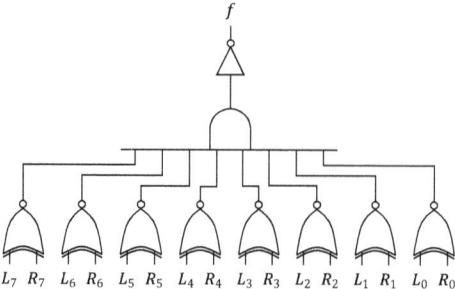

Figure 2.7: A logic representation of the negated equality-comparator unit $\overline{\texttt{COMP}}$ in Fig. 2.5.

designer to select the *optimization methods* and *effort levels*. The designer may also *enable or disable the restructuring* of the logic components and networks.

- Technology mapping: The logic representation is mapped into instances of a cell library, which is a set of primitive logic gates [14]. This step is also called 'cell-library binding'. The library includes combinational, sequential, and interface elements, with their characteristics such as area, delay, and load capacity. For FPGAs, the library can be defined implicitly, e.g., the virtual library of the look-up table is represented by all logic functions that can be realized by the tables [14]. Two main categories of binding approaches are heuristic and rule-based. The designer can control this step by providing manual *binding rules* or *cell selections*.

- Technology-dependent optimization: The resulting implementation is further optimized, taking into account the technology-dependent characteristics of the components, such as area, delay, and load capacity, that are determined during technology mapping. The optimization is usually performed by a variety of transformation techniques, such as gate sizing, Vt swapping, cell replication, buffer optimization, restructuring, remapping, and pin permutation [112, 113]. The designer may decide which *optimization techniques* to employ, which *objectives* to pursue, and how much *effort* to use. They may also pass *arguments* to the optimization algorithms via design parameters.

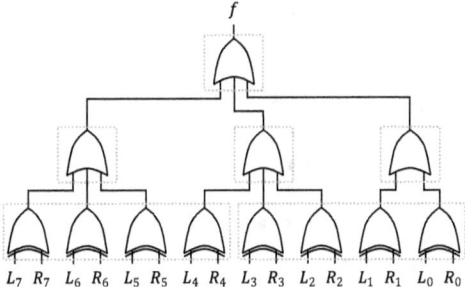

Figure 2.8: An example of an optimized implementation of the logic network in Fig. 2.7. The green dotted boxes represent bound cells from the technology library.

Fig. 2.8 illustrates an example of an optimized implementation of the logic representation for $\overline{\text{COMP}}$ shown in Fig. 2.7. The green dotted boxes indicate the cells from the library that are bound to the logic gates. The final implementation is described in a netlist, which contains the cells and connections between them. The netlist may be presented in text or schematic.

After each step or the entire process of LS, validation is performed to confirm the functional correctness of the implementation.

2.2.3 Physical Design

Fig. 2.9 illustrates a typical design process with PD. The PD tool or tool-chain translates a gate-level specification (described in a netlist) into a physical layout for integrated circuits, or into a configuration bitstream for FPGAs. While the presented abstract flow generally applies to both integrated circuit design and FPGA configuration, design flows for FPGAs usually consist of less number of stages, address smaller degree of freedom, and consequently, take less time for the design and optimization.

- Partitioning: To solve the complex PD problem efficiently, a large netlist is partitioned into smaller pieces that can be individually placed on a portion of a large chip or on an FPGA in a multi-FPGA system. The circuit partitioning problem is an NP-hard combinatorial problem; hence, PD tools usually rely on heuristic algorithms such as the

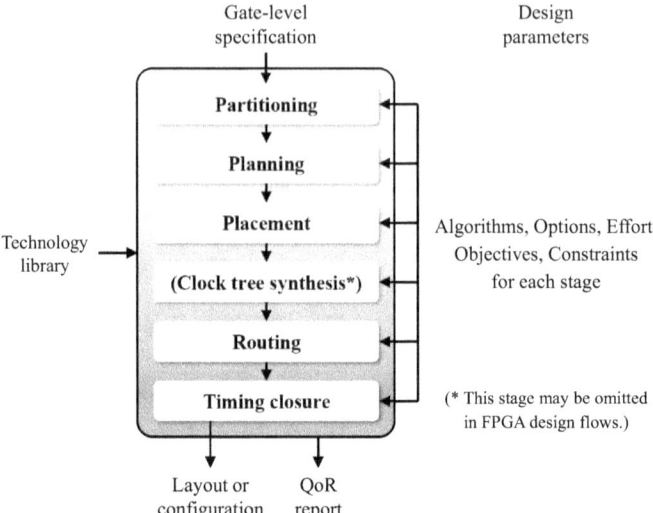

Figure 2.9: A typical design process with a PD tool or tool-chain that translates a gate-level specification into a physical layout (for integrated circuits) or configuration bitstream (for FPGAs). Each stage may involve the solution of intractable optimization problems and their execution can be guided by the design parameters.

Kernighan-Lin algorithm, the Fiduccia-Mattheyses algorithm, simulated annealing, or genetic algorithms [114].

- Planning: Before the core placement and routing, planning places periphery elements and establishes internal design constraints. Major substages of planning include floor-planning, pin planning, power planning, and clock planning. Floorplanning assigns dimensions and locations to large modules (clusters of logic with a known area) or to circuit partitions from the previous stage. The modules or partitions with assigned shape and location are called blocks. Pin planning defines the connectivity with all periphery elements such as external ports and interfaces. Power planning builds (for integrated circuits) or configures (for FPGAs) the power supply network. For FPGAs, clock planning configures the clock resources to distribute clocks across the system.

For integrated circuits, clock trees are usually synthesized after placement.

In VLSI design, especially floorplanning is a critical problem as it determines the performance, size, yield and reliability of chips [115]. Since it is another NP-hard combinatorial problem, many heuristic approaches have been applied including simulated annealing, genetic algorithms, particle swarm optimization, and ant colony optimization [116].

- Placement: After partitioning and planning, placement determines the spatial locations of cells or logic elements within each block (from the previous stage) while addressing the optimization objectives such as minimizing the total length of connections between elements (for routing) [15]. Techniques for placement, which is also an NP-hard problem, include partitioning-based algorithms, quadratic placement, force-directed placement, simulated annealing, and nonlinear optimization [15].

- Clock tree synthesis: A clock tree is generated for each clock domain of the system. The clock signal maintains the synchronization of all components in a clock domain, while different domains may run at different frequencies. Advanced FPGAs by default provide a few clock domains (configured in clock planning), but if the specification includes more clock domains, then clock tree synthesis is performed.

  The optimization objectives in clock tree synthesis include minimizing the clock skew (the maximum difference in clock signal arrival times) and minimizing the power consumption (because clocks are the major source of power consumption [117]) [15]. Since skew optimization requires highly accurate timing analysis which is usually infeasible, a common approach is to apply a sequence optimizations that include geometric tree construction, initial buffer insertion, buffer sizing, wire sizing, and wire snaking [15].

- Routing: After placement, routing (also called 'wiring') defines the interconnections. Global routing determines the regions traversed by the wires, followed by detailed routing which determines the specific location of the wires (including their layers and contacts) [14]. The optimization objectives include minimizing the total wire length and minimizing the critical path length (the length of the path with the longest combinational delay). Routing involves the solution of an NP-complete problem [118, 119], and it poses a major computational challenge in PD [15]. The applied approaches include iterative construction, genetic algorithms, ant colony optimization, and swarm intelligence [120, 121, 122, 123].

- Timing closure: The main constraints in PD are classified into three categories: technology constraints (e.g., minimum layout width), electrical constraints (e.g., maximum signal delay), and geometry constraints (e.g., boundaries provided by the designer) [15]. Timing closure is an optimization process of satisfying the timing constraints, which belong to the second category, through the layout optimizations and netlist modifications [15].

After the layout or configuration is generated, it must be fully verified to ensure the electrical and logical correctness [15]. The physical layout is usually in the GDSII stream format, and the FPGA configuration is in a bitstream.

Each stage of PD addressed above is related to one or more computationally intractable optimization problems. Design parameters for PD may determine the optimization algorithms, algorithm options, effort levels, objectives, and constraints for each of the stages.

The next chapter addresses the DSE problem for industrial VLSI design flows.

Chapter 3: A Recommender System Approach for Industrial Logic Synthesis and Physical Design Flows

As modern server-class high-performance computer systems consist of extremely complex hardware components containing billions of transistors on a single integrated circuit, the design paradigm has shifted to block-based and synthesis-centric design methodologies. A major portion of the system is partitioned into many blocks of distinct functions, each of which is designed and synthesized separately. Each block, also referred as *macro*, goes through the advanced industrial synthesis flow spanning logic synthesis through physical design. This flow is controlled by various and numerous knobs, called *meta-parameters* in this chapter, that ultimately affect the performance and feasibility. One of the key challenges and opportunities to optimizing a macro design is in the huge number of meta-parameters and other macros. In this chapter, I present a novel perspective of a collaborative recommender system which learns from the collective records of macros to make a tailored recommendation of meta-parameters for each macro. The proposed method learns hidden features of the macros and meta-parameters from the records containing only the identifiers of macros and meta-parameters and the score values of performance and feasibility, extracted from the synthesis log files. This eliminates the need for sharing the macro specifications and implementations, which is confidential information, with the recommender system.

3.1 Design of High-Performance Processors

The main computing engine at the core of any modern computer server is a high-performance processor realized as a VLSI circuit, i.e. a semiconductor circuit that integrates a huge number of transistors into a single chip. State-of-the-art system-on-chip architectures

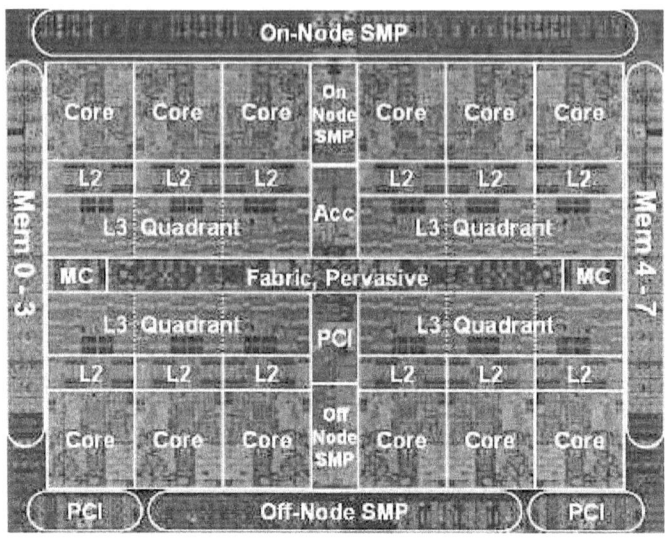

(a) A high-performance server-class chip with 12 processor cores.

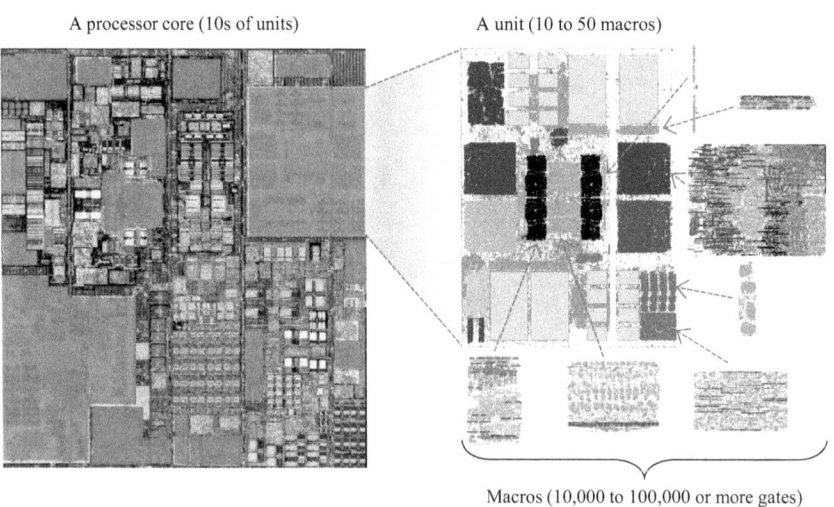

(b) Photographs of a processor core (left) and a unit consisting of many macros (right).

Figure 3.1: A hierarchical overview of a high-performance server-class chip, processor core, unit, and macros [124].

host billions of transistors on a single chip [125, 6, 8]. Such outstanding computational capabilities have been enabled by the progress of CAD tools for *logic synthesis and physical design* (LSPD), which have allowed hardware designers to cope with the remarkably growing complexity of VLSI design. The VLSI design process is structured along a sequence of refinement steps from higher levels of abstraction down to the detailed levels of circuit design. Hardware designers first specify the functionality of digital circuits with HDLs, such as Verilog [12] and VHDL [13], and then employ an *LSPD flow* which processes the circuit specification through a sequence of steps that include logic synthesis, physical placement, and routing, which have been introduced in Chapter 2.

In order to further handle the design complexity and allow CAD tools to run effectively, the specification of a complex circuit is typically partitioned into a set of many modules hierarchically. A high-performance processor typically consists of multiple processor cores, i.e., the main compute engines, surrounded by chip-level logic and memories [126, 6, 127]. Fig. 3.1(a) shows a photograph of a server-class processor chip containing 12 processor cores [124]. A core often consists of hundreds of macros. One of those cores is shown in Fig. 3.1(b) on the left, and one of its units is magnified on the right. A unit within a processor core is a level of hierarchy encapsulating 10 to 50 unique macros. The macros, shown around the unit in Fig. 3.1(b) on the right, are at the lowest level of hierarchy, consisting of 10,000 to 100,000, or even more, logic gates. Given the area and timing constraints, each macro is separately designed, synthesized, and optimized by a dedicated designer.

It is one of the main tasks performed by professional logic and physical designers to optimize the macros by *tuning* the LSPD flow. As most of the LSPD steps require the solution of many intractable (NP-hard) problems at a very large scale, it is infeasible for the CAD tools to automatically generate a final design that presents optimal values for multiple quality-of-result (QoR) metrics of interest, e.g., delay, power dissipation, routability, and area utilization. Furthermore, many of these metrics are inversely affected by design choices. For instance, increasing the processor performance by reducing the circuit delay typically comes

Table 3.1: Examples of *LSPD parameters*. These meta-parameters were activated as a result of the DSE for an exemplary macro.

LSPD parameter	Synthesis, placement, and optimization options
dpm	Area recovery and optimization after placement
fogs	Resizing late in the flow with accurate timing
latup	Allow upsizing of latches for timing
lpopt	Use a specific low-power optimization algorithm
sprd123	Spread out the logic during optimization steps

at the expensive cost of larger occupation of silicon area. CAD tools also need to be flexible to handle various types of logic functionality, making it difficult to rely on a single algorithm for all macro specifications. These challenges have led advanced LSPD flows to provide a variety of *meta-parameters* that affect the execution of CAD algorithms within the flow and, ultimately, impact the QoR. Table 3.1 provides an example of a few meta-parameters, also called LSPD parameters, from an industrial LSPD flow addressed throughout this chapter. Since advanced LSPD flows may have hundreds, or even thousands of parameters, it is an extremely complex task for the designers to configure those parameters for each macro.

While experienced designers may still manually tune parameters, automated parameter-tuning systems have recently emerged for LSPD and FPGA flows [26, 128, 129, 130]. Previously proposed systems for tuning CAD flows rely on iterative or adaptive online tuning algorithms that have significant runtime, disk space, and total compute resource costs. More recently researchers have focused on reducing iteration counts by parallelizing the CAD flow tuning algorithms: e.g. Xu et al. presented a distributed autotuning framework for optimizing FPGA designs [128], while Ziegler et al. presented a synthesis-parameter tuning system for VLSI designs that requires three to five iterations for each macro [26]. However, for industrial large-scale design efforts, there is a need to further reduce the parameter tuning costs. For instance, during a high-performance server design cycle, there may be hundreds of macros that need to be individually tuned, and the CAD tool input data may change frequently.[1] Thus, even effective iterative tuning systems can stress industrial compute clusters and design schedules. For the next level of parameter tuning efficiency, I (with M. Ziegler and L. Carloni) address the problem of AI-augmented tuning of the industrial LSPD flows for high-performance processors [46, 47].

3.2 Industrial LSPD Flows for High-Performance Processors

Fig. 3.2 shows a high-level diagram of an LSPD flow for industrial high-performance processors. The LSPD tool-chain takes as input a macro specification (RTL, timing requirements, physical boundary) and a configuration of LSPD parameters. The flow steps can be grouped into two main phases. The first phase performs a sequence of steps including logic synthesis, physical placement, clock tree synthesis, and post-placement optimization. Following these steps, key QoR metrics such as timing, power, and congestion (for routability) are reported based on estimated wire lengths, and these typically track well with the final QoR. Thus, designers often optimize QoR by tuning various LSPD parameters using Phase-1 QoR metrics as guidance in the process of *design-space exploration (DSE)*.[2] After the Phase-1 DSE, the second phase of the LSPD flow is executed to produce the final physical layout.

The target LSPD flow provides about 400 binary meta-parameters. When one meta-parameter is activated (i.e. is set to *True*), a group of synthesis, placement, and/or optimization parameters are set to specific values. A *scenario* refers to a configuration of all those LSPD parameters. With 400 binary parameters, the design space of a macro corresponds to 2^{400} different physical implementations that each could be synthesized for this macro with one scenario. The goal of the DSE process is to locate one or more high-quality (*near-optimal*) scenarios.[3] For this DSE task, an iterative parameter tuning flow, shown

---

[1] Industrial processor designs often follow synchronized LSPD version release schedules, e.g., a weekly or bi-weekly cadence.

[2] For the target LSPD flow addressed in this chapter, Phase-2 steps are computationally expensive, motivating the use of Phase-1 QoR metrics for DSE. Note that Phase-2 QoR metrics could also be used for DSE with lower Phase-2 overheads.

[3] The term *near-optimal* is used since the parameter tuning task is a black-box optimization problem and

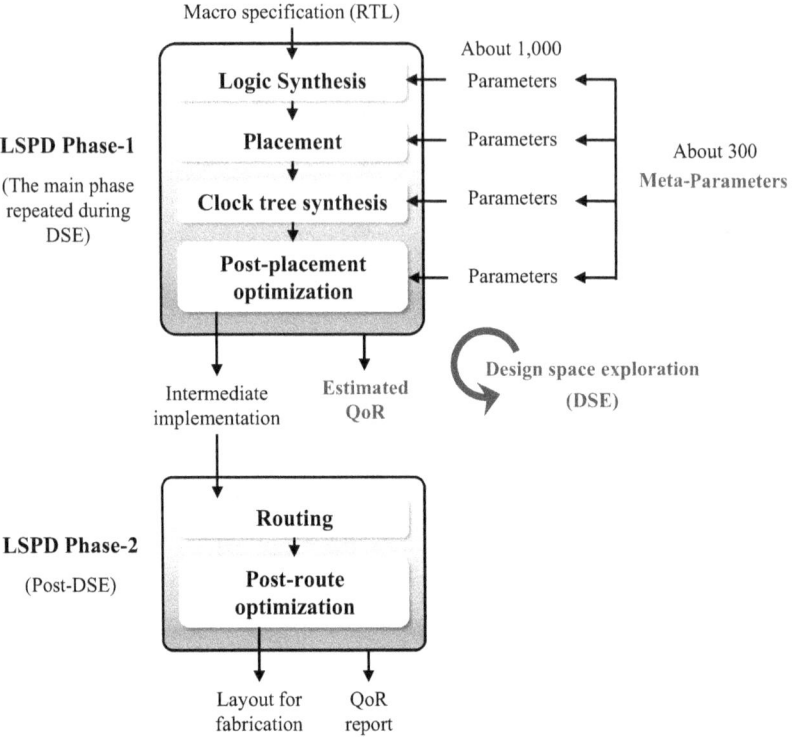

Figure 3.2: An LSPD flow deployed in an industrial environment for designing server-class high-performance processors.

in Fig. 3.3, has been employed to complete the design of multiple generations of industrial server-class processor chips.

As an example of iterative parameter tuning employed for prior processors, the design of a double-precision floating-point pipeline macro is considered. This macro contains 75,000 logic gates and takes 8 hours on average to be processed through the LSPD flow when deployed in an industrial environment targeting a 14nm semiconductor technology process (similar to the processes used in [125, 6, 8]). During five iterations of the parameter tuning

---

the design space is too large to perform an exhaustive search or to verify that an optimal solution is found. In practice, the goal of DSE is to locate solutions that provide notable improvements, rather than a precisely optimal solution.

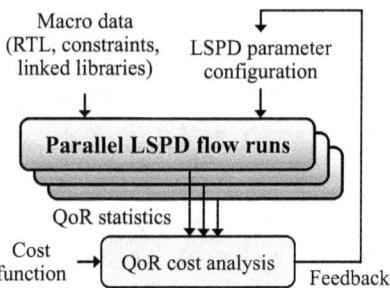

Figure 3.3: DSE with an iterative parameter tuning flow.

process, 173 LSPD scenarios with different parameter configurations have been applied, i.e., each iteration includes parallel execution of multiple scenarios. Table 3.1 reports the parameters of the top scenario determined through this process. While this iterative process has proven effective for many production processor designs, the overhead is still considerable, i.e., 173x compute resources and at least 5x runtime (latency). This overhead implies two important aspects of the target problem. First, it is significant to reduce the computational and runtime overhead by reducing the number of LSPD flow runs. Second, the top scenarios vary for the synthesized macros, prompting the need for multiple iterations of the tuning of parameter configurations. To reduce these iterations, it is critical to characterize each macro, especially with respect to its relationship with the parameters or scenarios. These motivate the research on applying machine learning to the target problem.

3.3 Opportunities for Machine Learning: LSPD Results Archive

The iterative tuning flow described in the previous subsection includes a background process that stores the data that are produced during each tuning run into an *archive*. As shown in Fig. 3.4, the archive of LSPD results consists of the (*Input: macro, scenario; Output: QoR*)–tuples from macros in multiple product families of high-performance processors, and over multiple design generations of these families. In total, the archive currently contains data from over 300,000 LSPD flow runs, from 1000s of macros across 22nm, 14nm, and 7nm

Input		Output (normalized QoR)				
Macro	Scenario	Slack 1	Slack 2	Slack 3	Power	Congestion
m_1	1000⋯0	0.42	0.56	0.34	0.88	0.76
	0110⋯0	0.89	0.87	0.68	0.75	0.60
	1010⋯1	0.92	0.84	0.56	0.65	0.54
	0101⋯1	0.27	0.30	0.40	0.45	0.63
	⋮	⋮	⋮	⋮	⋮	⋮
m_2	1000⋯0	0.34	0.22	0.50	0.56	0.83
	1011⋯0	0.51	0.63	0.74	0.66	0.77
	⋮	⋮	⋮	⋮	⋮	⋮
⋮	⋮	⋮	⋮	⋮	⋮	⋮

LSPD results Archive

Figure 3.4: An exemplary illustration of the LSPD results archive.

technology nodes. The archived LSPD results can be employed as training data for machine learning. Overall, the use of the iterative tuning flow provides an essentially free training set, whereas training sets for many other applications are curated through tedious and often manual processes. It should also be noted that the goal of the iterative tuning flow is to improve the QoR of the macro being tuned, not to supply a training set. Thus, the archived data is truly a by-product of the iterative DSE.

Once a macro is run through the iterative tuning flow and has data captured in the archive, it is referred as a *legacy* macro, whereas a macro without archived data is called a *new* macro. In general, a new processor generation reuses (inherits) some logic from prior generations and contains legacy macros and new macros, i.e., a legacy macro reuses some amount of logic from a macro in prior generations. The amount of reuse can vary from nearly full logic reuse, e.g., when remapping to a new technology, to partial logic reuse, e.g., for a new architecture [131]. Some examples in varying levels of reuse models include the "Tick-Tock" model or "Process-Architecture-Optimization" model [131]. However, even in the case of a new architecture target, the design complexity of a server chip and the requirements

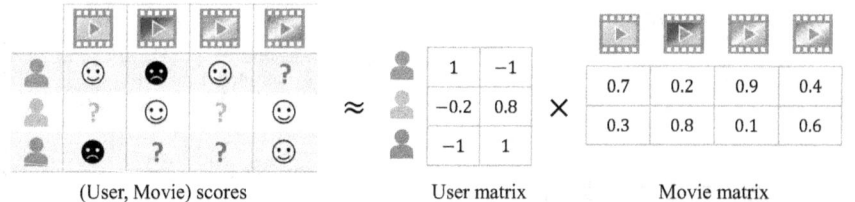

Figure 3.5: An example of a collaborative movie recommender system.

of supporting legacy code will result in a sizable amount of logic reuse. As a result of logic reuse, many macros within the new chip have the same or similar logic content as prior generations. Thus, in this chapter, the macros are categorized into previously observed macros (legacy macros) and unobserved macros (new macros). Other unobserved macros in the new generation processors are considered as new macros. When starting a new chip design, many macros are classified as legacy macros from observations in prior chips. Over the course of a chip design project, new macros are reclassified as legacy macros after they are iteratively tuned and added to the archive.

3.4 Relevant Machine Learning Approaches: Recommender Systems

Recommender systems predict the affinity between each user and items, such as movies, music, restaurants, shopping items, or posts on social network services, to make personalized recommendations [132, 133]. The application of recommender systems to complex engineering tasks is a new and interesting avenue of research with a potential for significant impact. In the area of software engineering, several systems have been proposed to assist developers in a range of activities [134, 135].

There are two main paradigms for recommender systems: content filtering and collaborative filtering. The content filtering approach analyzes the content, and thus heavily depends on the availability and performance of the analysis methods. On the other hand, the collaborative filtering approach exploits the collected information on how each user has reacted to each item. Since this approach mainly observes the users' reactions, it can be exploited

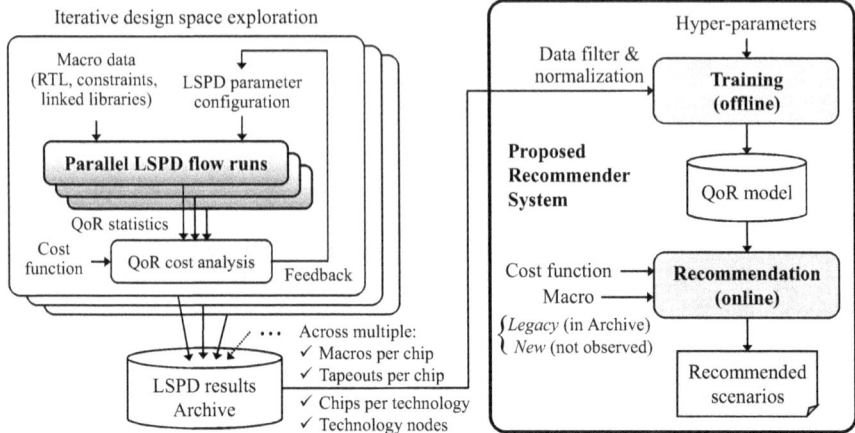

Figure 3.6: Overview of the LSPD tuning process, data archive, and proposed recommender system.

without further processing of the content. For instance, Fig. 3.5 shows a collaborative recommender system for movies that is based on the technique of matrix factorization [132]. The (user, movie) matrix, consisting of the observed movie ratings by the users, can be factorized into two smaller matrices, namely the user matrix and movie matrix, that represent hidden properties of the users and movies, respectively. By taking the product of these two matrices, it is possible to predict the unobserved movie ratings.

For the problem of LSPD parameter recommendation, I propose an analogy between the LSPD flow scenarios and the items (movies); between the macros and the users; and between the LSPD QoR and the users' reactions (movie ratings).

3.5 Proposed Approach: Collaborative Recommendation with Tensor Decomposition

Fig. 3.6 shows a high-level diagram of the proposed recommender system as well as the interactions with the archive and iterative tuning flow. The proposed system consists of two modules: (1) the *offline learning module* and (2) the *online recommendation module*.

The offline learning module trains a QoR prediction model using the LSPD results archive and the collaborative filtering approach. The online recommendation module takes as input the learned model, the target macro (the macro name for a legacy macro or sample LSPD results for a new macro), the QoR cost function or weight vector, and the number of scenario recommendations to generate. The module makes inferences using the given model and finally returns the requested number of recommended scenarios.

The recommender system's performance can be limited due to (1) the limited expressiveness of the model, (2) the sparsity of training data with respect to the huge search space, and (3) the complex nature of the problem, e.g., the existence of macro-specific or designer-specific parameters that the recommender system cannot address. In some cases, the performance can be improved by combining machine-generated scenarios with a design expert's input scenario (recorded in the archive for legacy macros). *The experimental results show that the collaboration between the recommender system and the design experts could lead to a QoR that is not achievable by either of them working solely.*

3.5.1 Offline Learning Module

The offline learning module leverages the LSPD results archive described in Sec. 3.3 in order to learn the affinity between the macros (*users*) and the LSPD flow scenarios (*items*). To describe this problem precisely, I formally define the system model as follows.

System Model and Problem Statement

Let $\mathcal{M}$ be a set of d macros: $\mathcal{M} = \{m_1, \cdots, m_d\}$, where m_i is a symbolic representation, e.g., the macro's name or index. Let $\mathcal{P}$ be a set of n binary (meta) parameters p_j. That is, $\mathcal{P} = \{p_1, \cdots, p_n\}$. A scenario s is a subset of $\mathcal{P}$, i.e., selected parameters that are set to *True*, while others are set to *False*. Then, $\boldsymbol{QoR}$ is defined as a function that maps a (*macro, scenario*)-pair to normalized QoR scores in ℓ metrics, presented as a real-valued ℓ-dimensional vector:

$$QoR(m, s) = (q_1, \cdots, q_\ell) \in [0, 1]^\ell, \; m \in \mathcal{M}, \; s \subseteq \mathcal{P}. \tag{3.1}$$

Unlike many other recommender systems where all users' ratings are given in a fixed range, e.g., from 1 to 5 stars, the evaluated QoR scores (e.g., timing, power) are distributed over different ranges of values depending on both the metrics and the macros. Let s^* be the most commonly applied scenario across all macros in the archive. The evaluated QoR score QoR_k^{ev} of the k-th metric ($1 \le k \le \ell$) for each macro m is normalized to a QoR score $QoR(m, s)_k$, that is in the range of $[0, 1]$, as follows:

$$QoR(m,s)_k = \begin{cases} \dfrac{QoR(m,s)_k^{ev} - \min_x QoR^{ev}(m,x)_k}{\max_x QoR^{ev}(m,x)_k - \min_x QoR^{ev}(m,x)_k}, \\ \text{if } s^* \text{ has not been applied to macro } m; \\[6pt] 0.5 + \dfrac{QoR^{ev}(m,s)_k - QoR^{ev}(m,s^*)_k}{2\max\{dmax(m,s,k), dmin(m,s,k)\}}, \\ \text{where } dmax(m,s,k) = \max_x QoR^{ev}(m,x)_k - QoR^{ev}(m,s^*)_k, \\ \text{and } dmin(m,s,k) = QoR^{ev}(m,s^*)_k - \min_x QoR^{ev}(m,x)_k, \\ \text{if } s^* \text{ has been applied to macro } m. \end{cases} \tag{3.2}$$

The archive in Fig. 3.6 contains QoR results from prior LSPD flow runs. For each macro m, let $S(m)$ denote the set of all scenarios that were applied during the DSE for m. An archive $\mathcal{A}$ (shown in Fig. 3.6) contains the $(m, s, QoR(m, s))$-tuples for all $m \in \mathcal{M}$ and $s \in S(m)$.

The first target problem is to find a prediction model F that approximates the QoR function, where F also maps a *(macro, scenario)*-pair to an ℓ-dimensional vector.

Problem 1 *Find a model F that minimizes*

$$\sum_{m \in \mathcal{M},\, s \subseteq \mathcal{P}} ||QoR(m,s) - F(m,s)||^2. \qquad (3.3)$$

In the above problem, the goal is to minimize the sum of L^2 distances between $QoR(m,s)$ and $F(m,s)$ for all macros m and scenarios s. However, for scenarios $s \notin S(m)$, the golden $QoR(m,s)$ values are unknown. Thus, the offline learning module aims to minimize the distances between $QoR(m,s)$ and $F(m,s)$ only for the scenarios recorded in the archive $\mathcal{A}$, which acts as the training data for machine learning.

Problem 2 *Given an archive $\mathcal{A}$, find a model F that minimizes*

$$\sum_{(m,s,QoR(m,s)) \in \mathcal{A}} ||QoR(m,s) - F(m,s)||^2. \qquad (3.4)$$

This can be viewed as a regression problem, attempting to predict the QoR values. One critical challenge is the lack of information regarding the input macro m and scenario s. A full specification of a macro is a collection of the designer's description, constraints, and linked libraries, that are neither easily available nor quantifiable.

Architecture of the Prediction Model

The aforementioned challenge is addressed by exploiting a collaborative filtering approach, which is widely used for recommender systems when the user information is not readily available [132]. For instance, a movie recommender system recommends a new movie to a user, based on this user's rating for other movies, and all other users' ratings. Let matrix A represent the movie ratings by all users, where A_{ij} represents user i's rating on movie j. Then, without further information, the system can learn latent features of each user and each movie, by factorizing matrix A into a user matrix B and the transpose of a movie matrix C, i.e., $A = B \cdot C^{\text{Tr}}$. This factorization can be done approximately when some elements of A are missing. After B and C are learned, a missing rating A_{ij} can be predicted as the (i, j)–element of $B \cdot C^{\text{Tr}}$ [132].

Our proposed architecture of the prediction model is motivated by the above approach for movie recommender systems, but it differs in addressing the following additional challenges.

C1. Unlike movies, the observed scenarios are very sparse. In the iterative parameter tuning example in Sec. 3.2, only 173 scenarios were observed for one macro, out of about 2^{400} scenarios. Moreover, sub-optimal scenarios for this macro were rarely observed while tuning parameters for other macros.

C2. While a movie rating prediction model outputs a single value for each (*user, movie*)–pair, the QoR prediction model outputs a vector with ℓ elements for each (*macro, scenario*)–pair.

To cope with **C1**, the prediction model factorizes the QoR information into a macro matrix, a parameter matrix, and the part that relates the latent information for (*macro, parameter*)–pairs to a *QoR* vector. On the other hand, **C2** indicates that ℓ individual models could be needed to predict each of the ℓ QoR metrics. Instead, I propose to construct one holistic model that predicts all ℓ metrics. This model can be described with a (*macro, parameter, metric*)–tensor in analogy to a (*user, movie*)–matrix. With this approach, it is possible reduce the number of variables describing the model,[4] and exploit all available information together to learn the latent features.

The proposed prediction model F describes the relationship between (*macro, scenario*)–pairs and their ℓ–dimensional QoR vectors by (1) a tensor decomposition approach for predicting missing values, and (2) an artificial neural network for the regression. Let T be a tensor whose (i, j, k)–element T_{ijk} represents an intermediate value of the k-th QoR metric for the (macro m_i, parameter p_j)–pair. These intermediate values, which are unknown

---
[4]The term 'variables' is more commonly referred as 'parameters' or 'weights' in other machine learning applications and recommender systems. In this chapter, I refer to them as 'variables' to avoid the confusion with 'LSPD parameters'.

at first, propagate through a neural network G that predicts the final QoR for a scenario. Thus, by the backward propagation of errors, the intermediate values can be adjusted, as well as other variables of G. Then, the tensor T containing the intermediate values can be decomposed into factor matrices containing the latent features.

Specifically, the tensor T has the shape of $|\mathcal{M}| \times (|\mathcal{P}|+1) \times \ell$, where $|\mathcal{M}|$ is the number of archived macros, and $|\mathcal{P}|+1$ is the number of parameters, including one pseudo-parameter that is always set to *True*. ℓ is the number of QoR metrics. By CP decomposition [136],[5] T is decomposed into the macro matrix M, parameter matrix P, QoR metric matrix Q, and one super-diagonal tensor of shape $h \times h \times h$, where h indicates the dimension of the latent features. The factor matrices M, P, and Q have dimensions of $|\mathcal{M}| \times h$, $(|\mathcal{P}|+1) \times h$, and $\ell \times h$, respectively. By this decomposition, an (i,j,k)–element of tensor T can be computed as

$$T_{ijk} = \sum_{\alpha=1}^{h} M_{i\alpha} \cdot P_{j\alpha} \cdot Q_{k\alpha}. \tag{3.5}$$

Given elements of the tensor T, a single-layer perceptron network G predicts the final QoR vectors [138]. That is, G can be expressed by a coefficient matrix R, a bias vector b, and an activation function, e.g., *tanh*. For an input vector v, it returns $G(v) = tanh_{ew}(v \cdot R + b)$, where $tanh_{ew}$ denotes an element-wise *tanh* function. Now, the input vector that corresponds to a (macro m_i, scenario s)–pair is defined as follows. For any parameter p_j, the vector $T_{ij:} = (T_{ij1}, \cdots, T_{ij\ell})$ represents intermediate QoR values for the (m_i, p_j)–pair. For notational simplicity, let $s(p)$ be 1 when the parameter p is in the scenario s, and 0 otherwise. The input vector is the concatenation of vectors $s(p_1) \cdot T_{i1:}, \cdots, s(p_n) \cdot T_{in:}$. Then, QoR for an (m_i, s)–pair can be predicted by $G(s(p_1) \cdot T_{i1:}, \cdots, s(p_n) \cdot T_{in:})$.

---

[5]CP and Tucker are two widely used methods for tensor decomposition. The acronym CP stands for 1) CANDECOMP (canonical decomposition) / PARAFAC (parallel factor analysis), or for 2) canonical polyadic (decomposition). Tucker is a generalization of CP, where the core tensor is not super-diagonal and contains hidden features [137]. With CP, it is possible to explicitly represent the latent information for each macro separately.

To summarize, the proposed model F is constructed as follows:

$$F(m_i, s) = G(s(p_1) \cdot T_{i1:}, \cdots, s(p_n) \cdot T_{in:}) \tag{3.6}$$

$$= tanh_{ew}((s(p_1) \cdot T_{i1:}, \cdots, s(p_n) \cdot T_{in:}) \cdot R + b) \tag{3.7}$$

Since T can be described by the latent feature matrices M, P, and Q, the model F can be written as

$$F(m_i, s; M, P, Q, R, b). \tag{3.8}$$

Here, F has two types of input: (1) the original input (macro m, scenario s) to F and (2) variables M, P, Q, R, b that describe how to compute F.

Training the Prediction Model

Training model F corresponds to learning its variables M, P, Q, R, and b. Let archives $\mathcal{A}$ and $\mathcal{B}$ contain the training and validation data, respectively. To solve the following problem, I use a stochastic gradient descent method [138]:

Problem 3 *Given $\mathcal{A}$, find model F's variables that minimize*

$$\sum_{(m,s,QoR(m,s))\in\mathcal{A}} ||QoR(m,s) - F(m,s)||^2 + \lambda_1 L^1(F) + \lambda_2 L^2(F). \tag{3.9}$$

To avoid overfitting F to $\mathcal{A}$, the L^1 and L^2 regularization terms $L^1(F)$ and $L^2(F)$ are added, each multiplied by small constants λ_1 and λ_2, respectively.[6] A trained model F is evaluated in terms of the validation error $\sum_{(m,s,QoR(m,s))\in\mathcal{B}} ||QoR(m,s) - F(m,s)||^2$. After a large number of training iterations, the offline learning module returns the model F with the smallest validation error.

---

[6] The L^1 regularization term is the sum of the absolute value of all variables v describing the model F, i.e., $L^1(F) = \sum_{v \in F} |v|$. Similarly, $L^2(F) = \sum_{v \in F} v^2$.

3.5.2 Online Recommendation Module

Given a trained QoR prediction model $F = F(m_i, s; M, P, Q, R, b)$, metric cost function or weights w, number t of scenarios, and target macro m, the online recommendation module returns t scenarios that are predicted to achieve near-optimal QoR scores (weighted by w) for m according to F. The predictions are made by the model $F(m, c; M, P, Q, A, b)$ that has been trained during the offline learning stage. Since the variables M, P, Q, A, b are fixed to some learned values, the output of F depends only on the macro m and configuration c.

For a legacy macro $m_i \in \mathcal{M}$, the $QoR(m_i, s)$ for any scenario s can be predicted by computing $F(m_i, s)$. Making an inference using this model F takes much less time than applying an LSPD flow (e.g., a few minutes vs. a number of hours).

For a new macro m^*, the recommendation module requires a number of sample LSPD results for this macro. In the case of a legacy macro $m_i \in \mathcal{M}$, the i-th row of the macro matrix M contains the latent features for this macro. Similarly, let μ denote the (unknown) latent feature vector for m^*. Then, $QoR(m^*, s)$ for a scenario s can be estimated by

$$F(m_1, s; \mu; P, Q, R, b). \tag{3.10}$$

In this model, only the values of μ are unknown, since the values of P, Q, R, and b are included in the learned model F. Thus, this μ can be learned using the model F and a sample LSPD results archive C.

Problem 4 *Given the model F and archive C, find μ that minimizes*

$$\sum_{(m^*, s, QoR(m^*, s)) \in C} ||QoR(m^*, s) - F(m_1, s; \mu; P, Q, R, b)||^2 + \beta. \tag{3.11}$$

β represents the sum of L^1 and L^2 regularization terms for μ. After μ is learned by the gradient descent method, the model F can be again used to make inferences for the new macro m^*.

After this process, the learned values of the variable μ can be considered as $M[i]$ in the legacy macro m_i's case. The following lemma states this.

Lemma 1 *For the model $F(m, c;\ M, P, Q, A, b)$, let's assume that the variables M, P, Q, A, b are set to certain values (as a result of training) such that* [7]

$$F(m, c;\ M, P, Q, A, b) \approx_{\mathcal{A}} QoR(m, c). \tag{3.12}$$

Let m_* be a new macro with the sample CAD results of

$$\mathcal{B} = \{(m_*, c, QoR(m_*, c)) | c \in C(m_*)\}. \tag{3.13}$$

If a vector μ satisfies

$$F(1, c;\ \mu;\ P, Q, A, b) \approx_{\mathcal{B}} QoR(m_*, c), \tag{3.14}$$

then the following holds:

$$F(m, c;\ M + \mu, P, Q, A, b) \approx_{\mathcal{A} \cup \mathcal{B}} QoR(m, c). \tag{3.15}$$

Thus, for a new macro, the online recommendation module can predict the QoR scores by learning the latent feature vector μ and using the model F.

3.6 Experimental Results

3.6.1 QoR Prediction Model

As described in Sec. 3.1, the LSPD results archive consists of the historical data for over 1,000 macros in multiple product families of high-performance processors, collected over a number of years and prior design efforts. For 250 binary meta LSPD parameters that are not

---
[7] $\approx_{\mathcal{A}}$ means values of the LHS are close to those of the RHS on set $\mathcal{A}$.

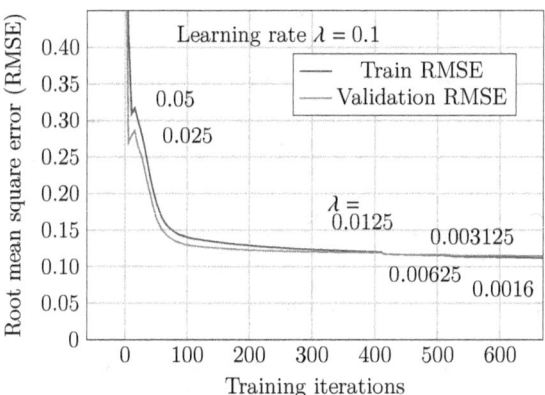

Figure 3.7: Train and validation error of the QoR prediction model.

too macro-specific or designer-specific, the archive contains about 300,000 (*Input: macro, scenario; Output: QoR*)-tuples, with 150,000 distinct scenarios.

For training, the archive is partitioned into a train set $\mathcal{A}$ (80%) and validation set $\mathcal{B}$ (20%). The QoR prediction model F was trained by 600 iterations of the gradient descent method, with the variables initialized to random values between −0.5 and 0.5. The trained model's accuracy is evaluated by the root mean square error (RMSE) on the train set:

$$train\ RMSE = \sqrt{\sum\nolimits_{(m,s)\in\mathcal{A}} ||F(m,s) - QoR(m,s)||^2/|\mathcal{A}|}. \tag{3.16}$$

The *validation RMSE* is defined similarly on the validation set $\mathcal{B}$. Fig. 3.7 shows the train and validation RMSE over the training iterations. Both RMSE values generally decrease as the number of iterations increases, with diminishing returns. The learning rate λ started from 0.1 and was decreased by a factor of two when the prediction accuracy (1−RMSE) did not improve over ten iterations.

The dimension h of the latent feature vectors (in Equation (3.5)) was set to 50 to achieve a good balance between the capability of the model and the applicability to a new macro. With higher h, the model can express a more complicated function. However, to learn the

Table 3.2: A representative set of five macros from industrial 14nm high-performance processors.

Macro name	Logic function	Logic gates	Runtime (hours)
FP	Floating-point pipeline	75,000	8.0
ECDT	Execution control & data transfer	45,000	6.2
IDEC	Instruction decode	210,000	21.6
ISC	Instruction sequencing control	77,000	13.1
LSC	L2 cache control & finite state machine	195,000	12.3

latent features of a new macro by solving Problem 4 in Sec. 3.5.2, at least as many sample LSPD runs as h are needed.

3.6.2 LSPD Parameter Recommendations

To evaluate the proposed recommender system, five macros in Table 3.2 are selected from a 14nm production processor. These macros, which perform distinct and critical logic functions, range in size from 45,000 to 210,000 logic gates. The average LSPD (Phase 1) runtime varies from 6.2 to 21.6 hours. These values are the averages, and it can take many more hours in the worst case.

QoR metrics of interest are the estimated worst slack, internal (register-to-register) slack, total negative slack, congestion score (routability), and total power. Since it is often very difficult to meet exactly the timing constraints for these macros during LSPD Phase 1, the goal of DSE has been set to minimize the weighted sum of QoR metrics, with a weight vector $w = [1, 2, 1, 3, 4]$ determined by design experts (according to the archive). Fig. 3.8 shows the average improvement of $\max_s w \cdot QoR(m, s)$ and the number of LSPD runs for the five target macros, achieved by the following methods.

- *Default*: The default setting of LSPD, where all parameters are set to *False*. This does not result in the worst QoR and it is the baseline for comparing the QoR of other scenarios. Other scenarios' QoR improvement is computed relative to this.

- *Sample*: About 50 parameters (each scenario contains one parameter) that were observed frequently and achieved high QoR according to the archive. The results from these scenarios are used by *Iterative* and *RS_New*.

- *Iterative*: DSE using a software program that iteratively improves the scenarios, following the approach proposed in [26].

- *RS_New*: 20 scenarios generated by the proposed method for a new macro, using results from 50 *Sample* runs.

- *Legacy (design expert's)*: The parameter configuration used by the designer who owned the macro for the production macro release. This may include settings of customized parameters that are effective only for the specific macro.

- *RS_Legacy*: 30 scenarios recommended by the proposed method for a legacy macro, each combined (by set-union) with *Legacy*.

The five macros are considered as new macros for *Default*, *Sample*, *Iterative*, and *RS_New*, and as legacy macros for *Legacy* and *RS_Legacy*. Fig. 3.8 and the 14nm section (top) of Table 3.3 show results from this experiment. The overall best approach is *RS_Legacy*, which combines the recommended parameters for legacy macros with the design expert's configuration. *RS_Legacy* is the only approach that closes the timing with a positive internal slack (a key metric) for all five macros. It also outperforms other methods on the other two slack metrics and is close to the best in terms of power and congestion scores. While the *Iterative* method eventually achieves a high QoR improvement, it runs more than 170 LSPD scenarios, taking 5 iterations. Although the proposed method *RS_New* shows a slightly lower improvement, it takes about 70 LSPD runs on average, achieving higher efficiency (the slope from the origin to the improvement point on the chart) than the *Iterative* method. Moreover, many scenarios by *RS_New* or *RS_Legacy* have never been observed in the archive or by other methods.

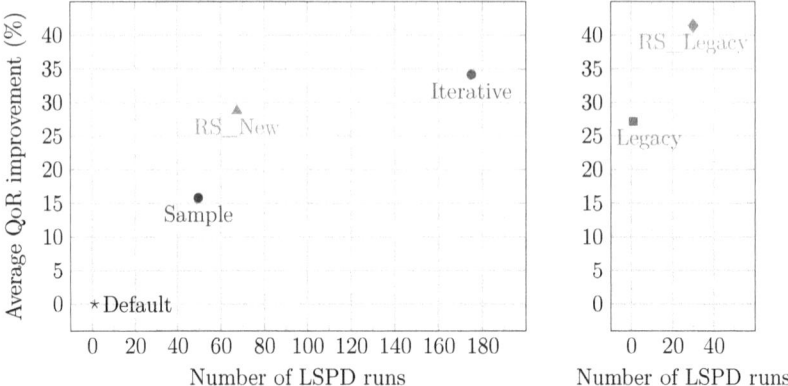

Figure 3.8: The QoR improvement and the number of LSPD runs by the six methods, averaged over the five macros in Table 3.2. The macros are considered as new macros for Default, Sample, Iterative, and RS_New methods (left), and as legacy macros for Legacy and RS_Legacy methods (right).

In a second experiment, the transfer-learning capability of the proposed system is explored by running a 7nm macro using scenarios recommended by a model trained with 14nm data [139]. This experiment is conducted on a 7nm version of the IDEC macro, which has similar logic functionality to the 14nm macro, but also some logic changes. The 7nm section (bottom) of Table 3.3 shows a comparison of the *Default* LSPD QoR and the *RS_Legacy14* approach, which is a combination of the recommended scenarios and the parameter configuration used for the final build of the 14nm version of the macro. *RS_Legacy14* provides a significant improvement in all three timing metrics, along with a small improvement in power and small degradation in congestion. Based on these results, it is believed that the proposed recommender system will provide a solid starting point for new chip design projects in future technologies.

3.7 Concluding Remarks

The proposed recommender system approach for DSE with industrial LSPD flows aims at reducing the high costs in VLSI design, especially for server-class high-performance pro-

Table 3.3: Sum of QoR metrics over the five 14nm macros (top), and the metrics for a 7nm macro (bottom). Positive slacks, lower congestion and power are preferred. 'a.u.' represents an arbitrary unit.

Technology	DSE Method	Worst slack (ps)	Internal slack (ps)	Total negative slack (ps)	Congestion score (a.u.)	Total power (a.u.)
14nm	*Default*	-350	-288	-474,886	549	303
	Iterative	-195	-84	-126,774	441	253
	RS_New	-200	-110	-167,936	457	265
	Legacy	-202	-53	-89,675	516	278
	RS_Legacy	-130	15	-19,691	458	266
7nm	*Default*	-53	-52	-60,047	83	187
	RS_Legacy14	-10	-13	-4,384	86	184

cessors. The proposed system learns the QoR prediction model using the LSPD archive and then uses it to generate scenario recommendations. In many cases, recommended scenarios are unique and have never been previously observed. Experimental results show that the proposed approach can reduce the computational cost of DSE, and assist designers to improve the QoR by recommending scenarios to combine with their own configurations.

The recommender system approach can be generally applied to large-scale DSE problems with a fixed scenario space for the target CAD tools or flows. With HLS, however, the scenario space varies depending on the specification. Thus, it is not feasible to construct a universal QoR prediction model with a fixed length of scenarios that can be applied to an arbitrary specification. The next chapter presents a transfer learning approach to address this problem.

Chapter 4: A Transfer Learning Approach for High-Level Synthesis

HLS raises the level of design abstraction, expedites the process of hardware design, and enriches the set of final designs by automatically translating a behavioral specification into a hardware implementation. Different implementations can be obtained with a variety of HLS knobs, such as loop unrolling or function inlining, applied to particular code regions of the specification. For the DSE of a single specification, conventional machine learning approaches can be employed to predict the performance and cost of the implementation from a configuration of the HLS knobs that are defined for the target specification. However, those approaches require a sufficient number of sample HLS runs for DSE of each specification. Can we apply what was learned from the DSE results of *different* specifications to assist the DSE of a *target* specification? This research problem is addressed in this chapter with a novel approach based on transfer learning. Transfer learning aims to improve the performance of a target learning task by reusing the knowledge obtained from different tasks or domains. I identify the challenges for AI-augmented DSE with HLS and present a series of five machine learning models for QoR prediction, in the order of evolution towards the proposed mixed-sharing multi-domain transfer learning.

4.1 Design of Hardware Accelerators: the HLS approach

Heterogeneous architectures have emerged as a response to the slowdown of technology scaling and the rise of diverse data-intensive workloads over the past couple of decades [140, 141, 76]. Specialized hardware accelerators deliver orders of magnitude performance improvement and energy advantage compared to general-purpose processors for applications

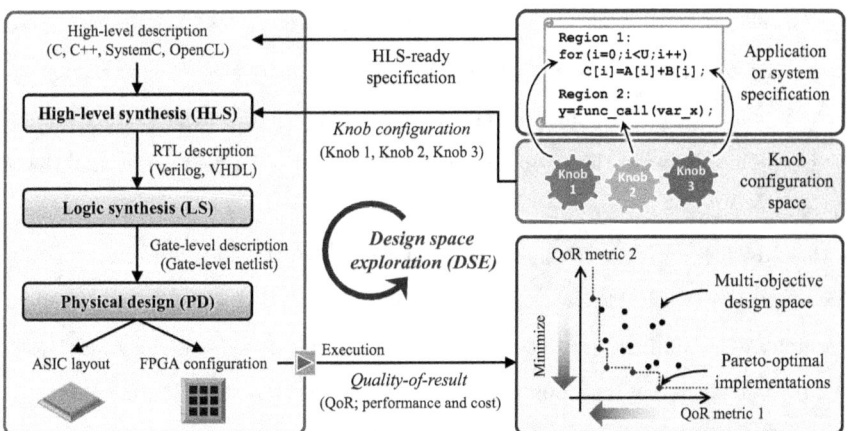

Figure 4.1: An overview of design-space exploration with high-level synthesis.

in a variety of domains [142]. However, design of specialized accelerators starting from a software application is a complex, expensive, and time-consuming task [76]. This can be dramatically facilitated by HLS flows that automatically translate high-level specifications into efficient implementations in ASICs or FPGAs, as depicted in Chapter 2.

Fig. 4.1 illustrates an elaborated overview of a design process with HLS from the design optimization perspective. For a target application or system, designers generate its behavioral specification (the top-right box shaded in yellow) either by implementing the target algorithm or by porting an existing high-level code into an HLS-ready version. While the specification is written in high-level languages, such as C, C++, SystemC [9], and OpenCL [10], state-of-the-art HLS tools are restricted to a subset of the high-level language functionality. For instance, most of the tools do not support dynamic memory allocation or recursion [143, 144]. Designers modify the high-level code to obtain a synthesizable and more optimized specification for HLS [145, 146, 147].

One high-level specification can be synthesized with different configurations of *HLS knobs* that direct HLS flows to generate alternative but functionally equivalent implementations. Most knobs define micro-architectural choices or synthesis options for particular code regions of the specification. In Fig. 4.1, the knob configuration space (the middle-right box shaded in green) consists of the value for each of the three knobs that determine the loop manipulation, function inlining, and array mapping options, respectively. The configuration of each knob can be specified either in the high-level description, or in a script file that controls the HLS flow.

The HLS flow processes the input specification and generates a hardware implementation that realizes the specified behavior. As shown in Fig. 4.1, the HLS tool translates a high-level specification into an RTL description, which is further transformed into an ASIC layout or an FPGA configuration bitstream via LS and PD (the left box shaded in blue). The knob configurations direct this HLS flow to generate alternative final implementations in terms of *QoR*, such as latency, area, and power. For instance, applying the unrolling option to a loop in the specification code generally results in a reduction of computational latency in exchange for an area increase.

A collection of such alternative implementations of a specification constitute a *design space* of that specification (the bottom-right box shaded in pink in Fig. 4.1). A design space includes implementations (to be) generated with all possible, feasible, or considered knob configurations. Designers *explore* the design space by running HLS flows with various knob configurations in order to obtain optimal implementations with respect to the multiple, often conflicting metrics of QoR. For the design of hardware accelerators as reusable soft IP, it is usually the goal of *DSE* to find the Pareto-optimal implementations in all QoR metrics of interest. Otherwise, designers may aim at finding a single optimal implementation with a specific objective and constraints.

4.2 Challenges for Design-Space Exploration with HLS

Fig. 4.2 summarizes DSE results for three applications from the Spector OpenCL FPGA benchmark suite: Sobel Filter, Breadth-First Search, and Merge Sort [148]. For each specification (the top yellow boxes), the knob configuration space is determined by a number of

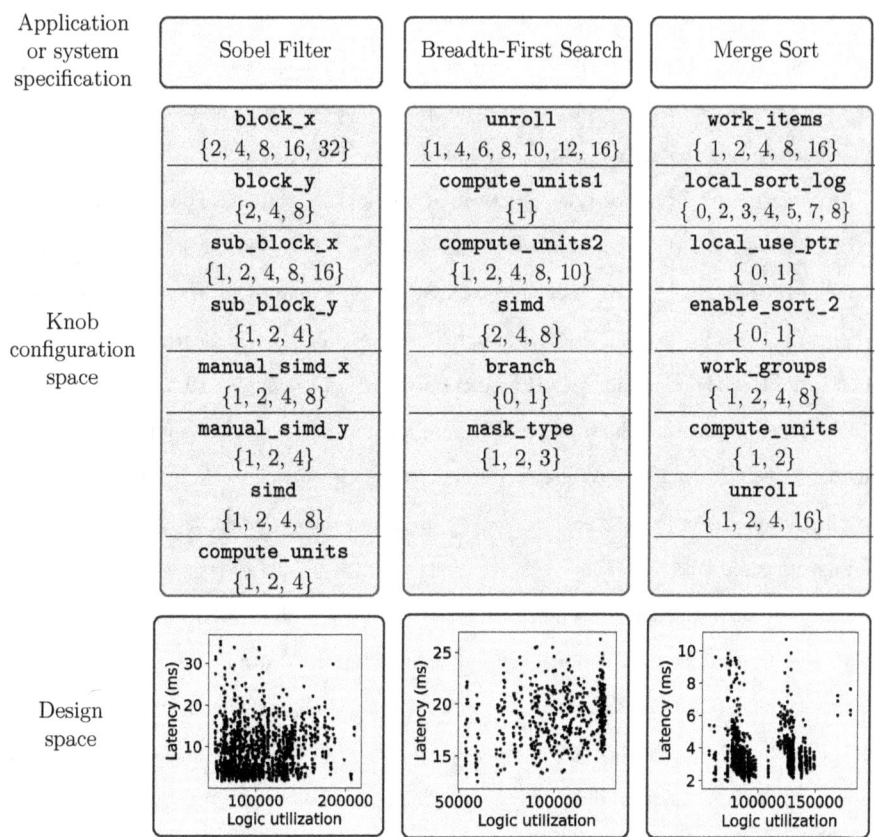

Figure 4.2: Design space exploration results for three applications in the Spector benchmark suite: Sobel Filter, Breadth-First Search, and Merge Sort [148].

configurable knobs, each with a set of values (the middle green boxes). The three specifications are associated with eight, six, and seven knobs, respectively. Each of those knobs has a distinct definition and a specific set of selectable values. The multi-objective design space for each specification, associated with the above knob configuration space, is presented with respect to two QoR metrics: the application latency, and logic resource utilization (the bottom pink boxes). The depicted implementation points were synthesized and evaluated by Gautier et al., the authors of the benchmark suite [148].

In practice, it can be costly, impractical, or infeasible to run HLS flows with every knob configuration since the total number of knob configurations grows exponentially with the number of individual knobs. For efficient DSE, a large number of approaches have been proposed [149, 150, 151, 152]. Recent approaches based on machine learning take the HLS flow as a blackbox and train a QoR prediction model using sampled HLS results [153, 154, 155]. These approaches, however, still require a sufficient number of samples to train the model with high accuracy. While this number depends on the specification and the knob configuration space, in the worst cases, 20% to 50% of the design space have been sampled and synthesized [153, 154, 155].

Conventional machine learning approaches train a separate QoR prediction model for each specification, because a model constructed for one specification cannot take input from a new specification that is associated with a different knob configuration space. As shown in Fig. 4.2, each specification has a different number of distinct knobs and a unique design space with diverse ranges and distributions of QoR. In this chapter, I investigate the following research problem: *Can we apply what was learned for previous specifications to aid the DSE of a new specification?* By reusing the learned knowledge across different specifications, it is expected to enhance the training performance and reduce the sample complexity.

Transfer learning attempts to achieve this goal. For a machine learning task with limited data, transfer learning approaches reuse the knowledge obtained from different yet related tasks with abundant data. For instance, neural network models trained for natural image classification can be transferred to aid the disease classification in medical images [156]. The new model for the disease classification consists of the pre-trained sub-network for feature extraction and a newly added layer for classification.

This chapter presents a novel transfer-learning approach for AI-augmented DSE with HLS. To the best of my knowledge, this is the first work proposing the application of transfer learning to HLS QoR prediction where different specifications have different knobs or synthesis options.

4.3 Challenges for Transfer Learning with HLS

Transfer learning aims to improve the performance of a *target* learning task by reusing the knowledge obtained for different but related *source* tasks or domains. The properties and characteristics of HLS-driven DSE pose three critical challenges in applying transfer learning:

- Both the input *domain* and output *range* of the learning problem vary across specifications. A QoR prediction model takes as input a knob configuration and outputs predicted QoR values. As shown in Fig. 4.2, the three specifications have a different number of knobs and distribution of realized QoR.

- Obtained knowledge for one application may include application-specific information. Since Sobel Filter, Breadth-First Search and Merge Sort have different levels and structures of parallelism, applying some common knobs may have different impacts on their QoR.

- The target application may contain its own properties which other applications did not exhibit. Hence, the obtained knowledge from source applications may be insufficient to fully describe and predict HLS results of the target application.

Each of the above challenges is addressed in this chapter as follows. First, an *internal* part of the prediction model from the source task is transferred. For a neural network model that predicts output QoR from an input knob configuration, the dimension of the input layer depends on the specification's knob configuration space. Hence, unlike the image classification transfer learning that transfers the intermediate representation learning part, the proposed approach transfers the regression learning part starting from an intermediate representation.

Second, a *multi-domain* transfer learning approach is proposed, where a common model is trained from multiple source domains. For instance, if DSE results for Breadth-First Search are available together with those for Sobel Filter in Fig. 4.2, a neural network model can be constructed such that the model contains two versions of the first hidden layer, one with eight elements for Sobel Filter, and the other with six elements for Breadth-First Search. This is in an attempt to extract effectively common knowledge between multiple source applications that is expected to be shared also with the target application.

Third, a *mixed-sharing* multi-domain transfer learning approach is proposed. In multi-task learning and transfer learning, *hard parameter sharing* refers to the sharing of a common model by multiple tasks [157]. In *soft parameter sharing*, each task has its own model and parameters, where some parameter values are shared across all tasks [158]. I propose a mixed-sharing approach to reflect the diversity of various source and target applications, as presented in the next section.

4.4 Proposed Approach: Towards Mixed-Sharing Multi-Domain Transfer Learning

This section presents a series of neural network models addressing the aforementioned challenges, in the order of evolution starting from a single-domain single-task learning towards the proposed mixed-sharing multi-domain transfer learning.

4.4.1 System Model and Problem Description

Let X denote the set of all configurations x of n HLS knobs defined for a given specification:

$$x = (x^1, \cdots, x^n) \in X \subset \mathbb{R}^n \tag{4.1}$$

Let QoR be a function that maps a knob configuration to the QoR values obtained by applying the target HLS flows:

$$QoR : X \to \mathbb{R}^m \tag{4.2}$$

$$QoR(x) = (QoR^1(x), \cdots, QoR^m(x)) \tag{4.3}$$

where m denotes the number of QoR metrics of interest. As shown in Fig. 4.2, the ranges of QoR values vary depending on the specification. Let $Train$ denote the set of knob configurations $x \in X$ with known QoR values, and $Test$ the set of those with unknown QoR values. A normalized QoR function $\widetilde{QoR}_{Train}$ returns the QoR values for $x \in Train$ normalized to a fixed interval, e.g., $[0,1]^m \subset \mathbb{R}^m$, where the normalization is performed separately for each QoR metric. When this function is applied to $x \in Test$, some of the resulting $\widetilde{QoR}_{Train}(x)$ values may be out of the original normalization interval. When $Train$ is obvious, we omit it from the notation $\widetilde{QoR}_{Train}$. The target problem for a given specification is to learn its $\widetilde{QoR}$ function, given a $Train$ set labeled with the observed QoR values:

Problem 5 *Given $Train \subset X$, find a prediction function $F : X \to \mathbb{R}^m$ that approximates $\widetilde{QoR}$:*

$$\arg\min_F \sum_{x \in X} ||F(x) - \widetilde{QoR}(x)||^2 \tag{4.4}$$

The goal of machine learning for classification and regression is to learn a label-prediction function, given an input *domain* (a set of knob configurations), output label space (the range of normalized QoR values), and training data (sampled DSE results). Recently, neural network models have been extensively used in machine learning tasks to represent the prediction functions. Inspired by the human brain, a neural network consists of processing layers that

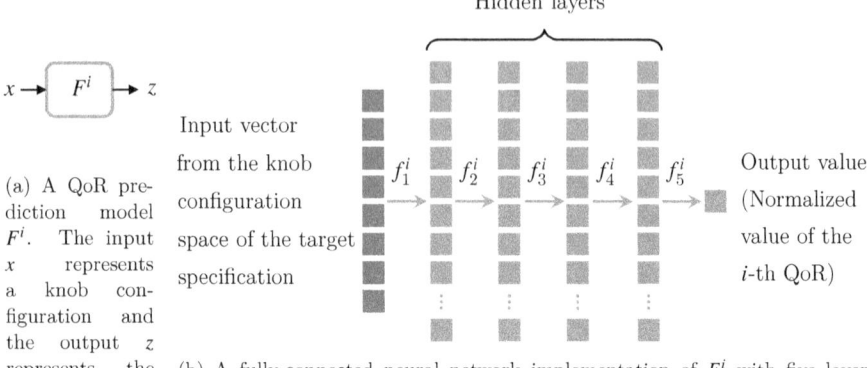

(a) A QoR prediction model F^i. The input x represents a knob configuration and the output z represents the predicted $\widetilde{QoR}^i$.

(b) A fully-connected neural network implementation of F^i with five layer functions f^i_j ($1 \leq j \leq 5$).

Figure 4.3: A predictive model F^i for $\widetilde{QoR}^i$ ($1 \leq i \leq m$) in single-task learning.

contain computation units called nodes or neurons [159]. By the universal approximation theorem, any continuous function on a compact set can be approximated by a fully-connected neural network [160, 161]. In this work, a fully-connected neural network model is proposed for HLS QoR prediction.

4.4.2 Single-Task Learning

In single-task learning, a single predictive model $F^i : X \to \mathbb{R}$ approximates a single unknown target function $\widetilde{QoR}^i$, as shown in Fig. 4.3 (a). A fully-connected neural network implementation of the abstract model is illustrated in Fig. 4.3 (b). A neural network consists of layers, and each layer contains nodes, depicted as small solid squares in the figure. Each node represents a single value, and the width of a layer is the number of nodes contained in it. The input layer represents a knob configuration x from the domain X. The j-th layer ℓ^i_j is computed with a function f^i_j that takes the previous layer as input and outputs a vector of dimension equal to the width of ℓ^i_j. Layer functions f^i_j are defined as follows:

$$f^i_j(y) = Activation(A^i_j y + b^i_j) \qquad (4.5)$$

where A_j^i is a weight matrix, b_j^i is a bias vector (of appropriate dimensions), and *Activation* denotes a nonlinear activation function such as hyperbolic tangent, sigmoid, rectified linear unit, or softmax. A neural network implementation of F^i with five layers, as shown in Fig. 4.3 (b), is a composition of the five layer functions f_j^i ($1 \leq j \leq 5$):

$$F^i(x) = (f_5^i \circ f_4^i \circ f_3^i \circ f_2^i \circ f_1^i)(x) = f_5^i(f_4^i(f_3^i(f_2^i(f_1^i(x))))) \tag{4.6}$$

The objective of the learning is to minimize the difference between the predicted QoR $F^i(x)$ and the actual QoR value $\widetilde{QoR}^i(x)$ for all knob settings x. Given a configuration set *Train*, Problem 5 can be re-written as follows:

$$\underset{F^i=(A_1^i,b_1^i,\cdots,A_5^i,b_5^i)}{\arg\min} \sum_{x \in Train} \| F^i(x) - \widetilde{QoR}^i(x) \|^2 \tag{4.7}$$

Stochastic gradient descent and its variants with optimization techniques have been demonstrated to solve effectively the above problem [162]. The L1 norm and squared L2 norm of the weights A_j^i multiplied by a small coefficient are often added to the objective function in Eq. (4.7) as regularization terms.

4.4.3 Multi-Task Learning

Instead of learning one model for each QoR metric as in Fig. 4.4 (a), multi-task learning attempts to improve the performance of multiple learning tasks by using some common knowledge contained in those tasks, as shown in Fig. 4.4 (b) [163]. Fig. 4.4 (c) illustrates a neural network implementation of the multi-task model G for m QoR metrics of interest, defined as follows:

$$G(x) = (G^1(x), \cdots, G^m(x)) \tag{4.8}$$

$$G^i(x) = (f_5^i \circ f_4^i \circ g_3 \circ g_2 \circ g_1)(x) = f_5^i(f_4^i(g_3(g_2(g_1(x))))) \tag{4.9}$$

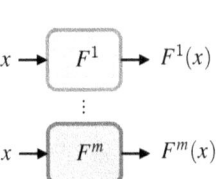

(a) Multiple single-task models $F^i, \cdots, F^m$. The input x represents a knob configuration and the output F^i represents the predicted $\widetilde{QoR}^i$.

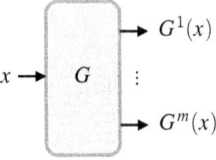

(b) A multi-task model G. The input x represents a knob configuration and the output $G^1(x), \cdots, G^m(x)$ represent the predicted $\widetilde{QoR}^1, \cdots, \widetilde{QoR}^m$, respectively.

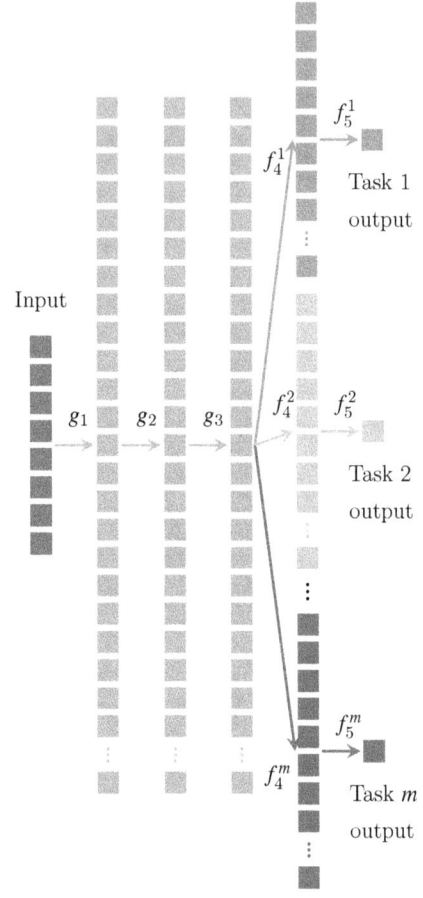

(c) A neural network implementation of G. A common sub-network (green layers) is connected to the task-specific ones (sky-blue, pink, and purple layers).

Figure 4.4: A predictive model G for $\widetilde{QoR}$ in multi-task learning.

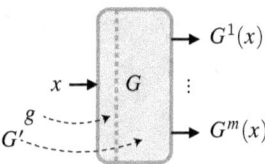
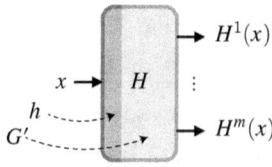

(a) A multi-task model G as a composition of two functions g and G' for the source task. g maps a knob configuration x into an intermediate representation, which is mapped to the predicted $\widetilde{QoR}^1, \cdots, \widetilde{QoR}^m$ by G' for the source specification.

(b) A transfer learning model H as a composition of two functions h and G' for the target task. h maps a knob configuration x into an intermediate representation, which is mapped to the predicted $\widetilde{QoR}^1, \cdots, \widetilde{QoR}^m$ by G' transferred from G in (a).

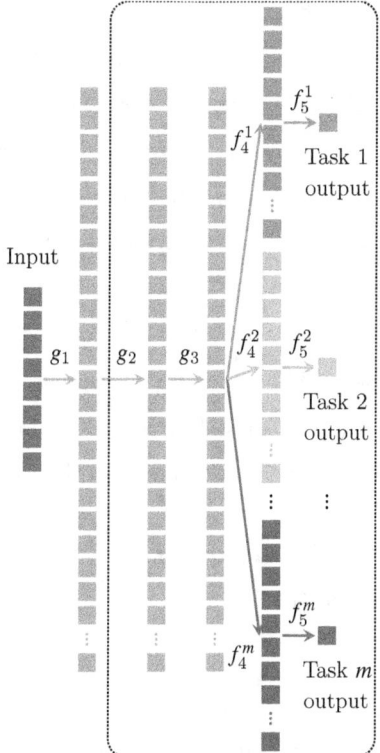
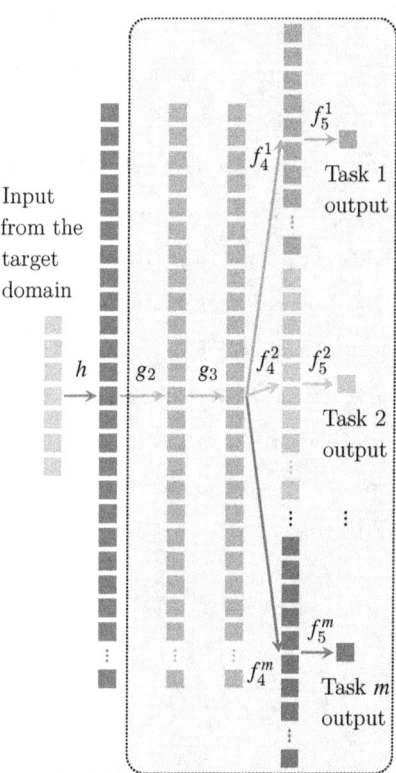

(c) A neural network implementation of G. This model is trained with the source specification, and its sub-network (in the dotted line) is transferred.

(d) A neural network for H. The sub-network of G is transferred to this model (in the shaded box). The first hidden (brown) layer is freshly trained.

Figure 4.5: A source model G and a target model H for cross-domain transfer learning.

where g_1, g_2, and g_3 are nonlinear functions for the first three hidden layers. The input for g_1 is a knob setting $x \in X$ for the target specification. The output of g_3 represents the common feature that is used as an input to $f_5^i \circ f_4^i$ for each task i.

From experiments, it has been observed that when the size of *Train* is large enough, single-task models can approximate the target function with higher accuracy on *Test* than multi-task ones, but when *Train* is relatively small, multi-task models outperform single-task ones.

4.4.4 Cross-Domain Transfer Learning

The QoR prediction model in Fig. 4.5 (a) learned for one specification can be transferred to have a different domain, as shown in Fig. 4.5 (b). More precisely, *a part of the neural network learned for the source task is transferred to be a part of another neural network for the target task.* The source model G can be described as a composition of two functions g and G', i.e., $G = G' \circ g$. Given a pre-trained multi-task model G, a target model H can be constructed as $G' \circ h$, where G' is transferred from G and h is a new function defined on the domain of H. Fig. 4.5 (c) and Fig. 4.5 (d) illustrate a neural network implementation of the source model G and the target model H, respectively. The dotted box in Fig. 4.5 (c) corresponds to G' that is transferred to the shaded box in Fig. 4.5 (d). Given the neural network of the source model G as in Eq. (4.8) and Eq. (4.9), a neural network of the target model H is defined as follows:

$$H(x) = (H^1(x), \cdots, H^m(x)) \qquad (4.10)$$

$$H^i(x) = (f_5^i \circ f_4^i \circ g_3 \circ g_2 \circ h)(x) = f_5^i(f_4^i(g_3(g_2(h(x))))) \qquad (4.11)$$

where h denotes the new nonlinear function in the first hidden layer (the brown layer in Fig. 4.5 (d)). Pre-trained functions g_2, g_3, f_4^i, and f_5^i (in the shaded box in Fig. 4.5 (d)) are transferred from G. The leftover part in G is its first hidden layer g_1. The domain of g_1 is the knob configuration space of the synthesized specification that G has been trained for. The codomain of g_1 is a vector space of a fixed dimension, which is the domain of g_2. The new function h is defined with the domain of the knob configuration space for the new target specification and its codomain is equal to that of g_1. Since this codomain coincides with the domain of g_2, the function composition of $g_2 \circ h$ is well-defined in the new model H. The transferred part determines how to compute the predicted QoR values from the intermediate feature and it remains fixed during training for the new target task. Only the new function h from the target domain to the intermediate feature space is learned, possibly with much smaller samples. The optimization problem can be expressed as follows:

$$\underset{h=(A_h,b_h)}{\arg\min} \sum_{x \in Train} \| H(x) - \widetilde{QoR}(x) \|^2 \qquad (4.12)$$

4.4.5 Multi-Domain Transfer Learning

Transfer learning aims to improve the performance of the target learning task by discovering and transferring latent or hidden knowledge from the source domain and task [164]. One of the main research topics in transfer learning is "what to transfer." Some knowledge is specific for individual domains or tasks, whereas some other common knowledge can be transferred to help improve the performance of the target task [139]. Thus, it is critical to identify such common knowledge, which is often latent. In an attempt to more effectively disentangle common latent knowledge from what is specific for the source domain and task, I propose a multi-domain transfer learning model that interacts with multiple source domains.

Fig. 4.6 (a) and Fig. 4.6 (b) illustrate the source model and the target model, respectively, of the proposed multi-domain transfer learning. In this model, it is assumed that HLS results for multiple source specifications are available for pre-training. For D source specifications with heterogeneous knob configuration spaces X_d ($1 \leq d \leq D$), the proposed multi-domain QoR prediction model P is defined as $P(d, x_d) = (P' \circ p_d)(x_d)$, where $x_d \in X_d$, and function

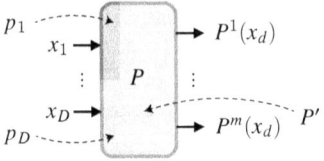

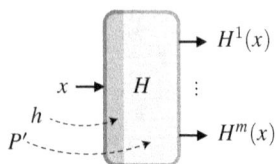

(a) A multi-domain multi-task model P for multiple source tasks. p_d ($1 \leq d \leq D$) maps an input x_d from the d-th source knob configuration space into an intermediate representation, which is mapped to the predicted $\widetilde{QoR}^1, \cdots, \widetilde{QoR}^m$ by P'.

(b) A transfer learning model H as a composition of two functions h and P' for the target task. This model is the same as in Fig. 4.5 (b), except that P' in this model is transferred from P in (a) on the left.

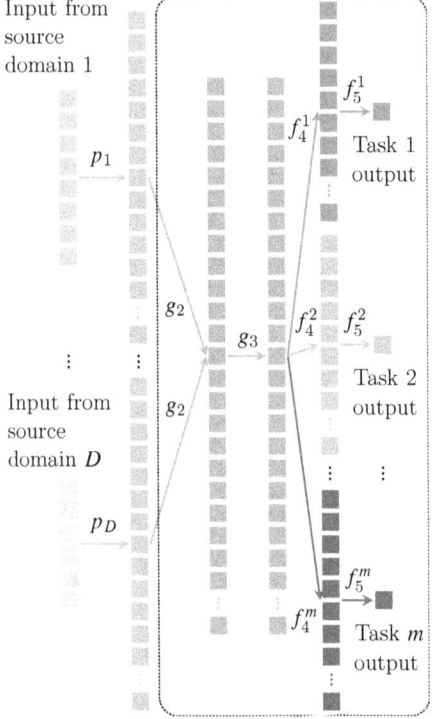

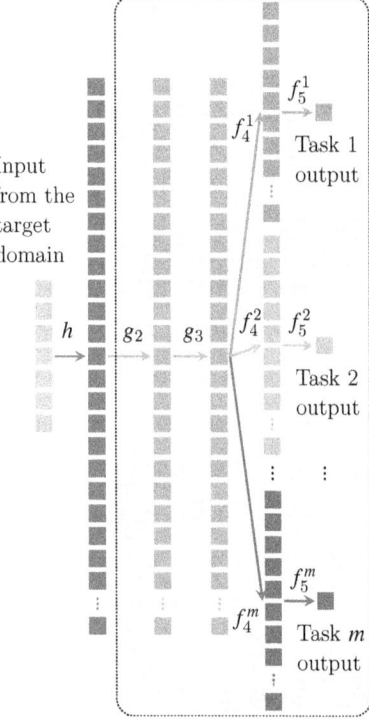

(c) A neural network implementation of P. This model is trained on multiple source domains. Then, the trained sub-network (in the dotted box) is transferred.

(d) A neural network for H. The sub-network of P is transferred to this model (in the shaded box). This neural network is also the same as in Fig. 4.5 (d).

Figure 4.6: A source model P and a target model H for multi-domain transfer learning.

p_d is defined on X_d. Function P' plays the fundamentally same role as G' in model G for cross-domain transfer learning (Fig. 4.5), but P' is trained with multiple source tasks. A neural network implementation of P, as illustrated in Fig. 4.6 (c), is defined as follows:

$$P(d, x_d) = (P^1(d, x_d), \cdots, P^m(d, x_d)), \ 1 \le d \le D, \ x_d \in X_d \qquad (4.13)$$

$$\begin{aligned} P^i(d, x_d) &= (f_5^i \circ f_4^i \circ g_3 \circ g_2 \circ p_d)(x_d) \\ &= f_5^i(f_4^i(g_3(g_2(p_d(x_d))))), \ x_d \in X_d \end{aligned} \qquad (4.14)$$

where p_d represents the individual feature function for specification d. The domain of each p_d is the knob configuration space for specification d, but their codomain is the common feature vector space with a fixed dimension, which is also the domain of the next layer function g_2. In this model, p_d functions for $d \ne 1$ have some similarities with h in the cross-domain transfer learning model H (in Fig. 4.5 (d)). However, whereas h and its inputs are not used for the pre-training of the rest of H (which has been transferred from G), all p_d functions and their inputs are used for training the entire model P. By exploring multiple source domains and individual feature functions simultaneously, the shared part of the model $f_5^i \circ f_4^i \circ g_3 \circ g_2$, grouped by the dotted box in Fig. 4.6 (c), is expected to extract common latent knowledge, while individual p_d functions are expected to interpret knowledge specific to each specification. Then, the shared part can be transferred to a new model for the target specification, as shown in the shaded box in Fig. 4.6 (d).

4.4.6 Mixed-Sharing Multi-Domain Transfer Learning

To further separate common knowledge from possibly application-specific and domain-specific knowledge, I propose another multi-domain multi-task model, illustrated in Fig. 4.7, that reconciles two types of parameter sharing: hard and soft. The models in Fig. 4.5 and Fig. 4.6 employ hard parameter sharing, where individual active networks for different

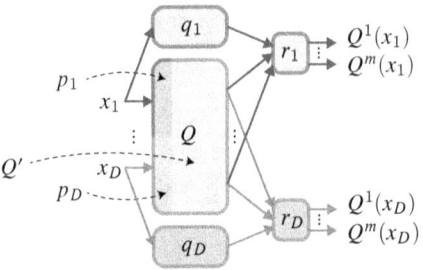
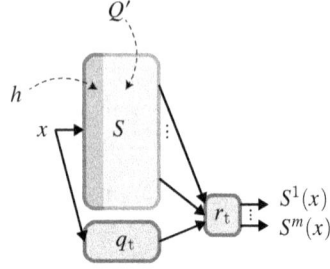

(a) A mixed-sharing multi-domain multi-task model Q for multiple source tasks. The input x_d ($1 \le d \le D$) for the d-th source task is processed in parallel by an auxiliary function q_d, and by p_d followed by Q'. The output from the two paths are passed to r_d, which outputs the final predicted $\widetilde{QoR}^1, \cdots, \widetilde{QoR}^m$ for x_d.

(b) A transfer learning model S for the target task. The input x is processed in parallel by q_t, and by h followed by Q'. The output from the two paths are passed to r_t, which generates the final output. Q' is transferred from Q in (a), whereas q_t and r_t are trained for the target task.

Figure 4.7: A source model P and a target model S for mixed-sharing multi-domain transfer learning with both hard and soft parameter sharing.

specifications share a common sub-network (the dotted box in (c) and the shaded box in (d) of each figure). In soft parameter sharing, each task has its own network and parameters where some parameter values are shared (the values are either identical or very similar) across those tasks [157, 158]. The proposed model Q incorporates both hard parameter sharing and a variant of soft parameter sharing, as shown in Fig. 4.7 (a):

$$Q(d, x_d) = r_d\Big((Q' \circ p_d)(x_d), q_d(x_d)\Big), \ 1 \le d \le D, \ x_d \in X_d \qquad (4.15)$$

where function p_d is defined on the knob configuration space X_d, function Q' predicts values of intermediate QoR, function q_d separately and independently predicts intermediate QoR, and function r_d takes in the two intermediate QoR predictions to output the final predicted $\widetilde{QoR}$ for x_d. Q' is shared by multiple source tasks, while p_d, q_d, and r_d are used only for specification d. The target model S for mixed-sharing transfer learning is shown in Fig. 4.7 (b):

$$S(x) = r_t\Big((Q' \circ h)(x), q_t(x)\Big), \ x \in X_t \qquad (4.16)$$

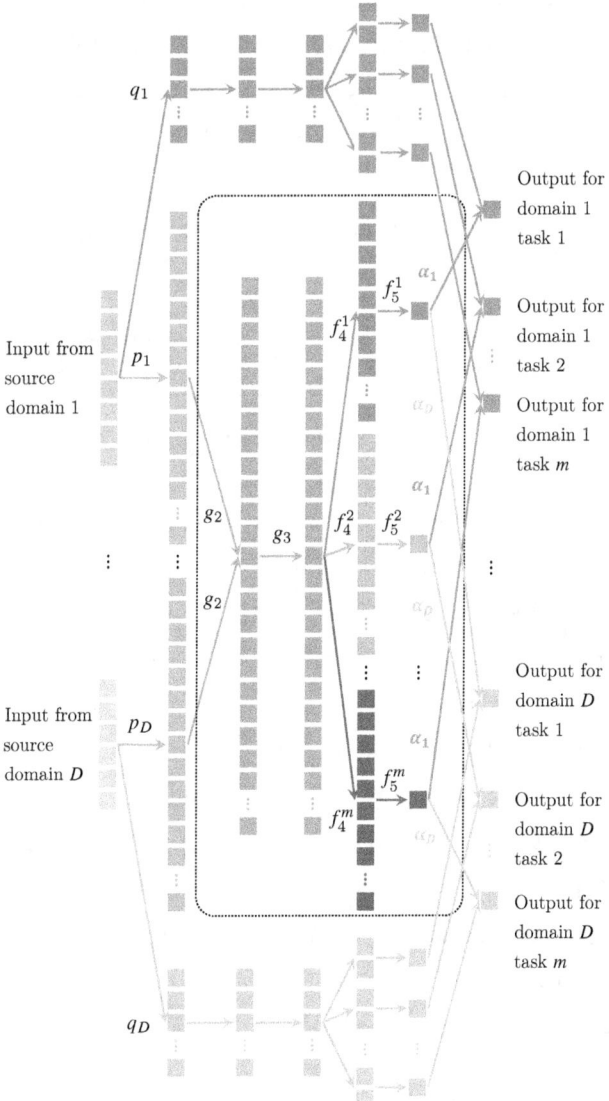

Figure 4.8: A neural network implementation of the mixed-sharing multi-domain model Q shown in Fig. 4.7 (a). The sub-network in the dotted box (Q') is transferred to the target model.

Here, X_t denotes the knob configuration space for the target specification, function Q' is transferred from model Q, and functions h, q_t, and r_t are defined for the target task.

Fig. 4.8 illustrates a neural network implementation of the source model Q shown in Fig. 4.7(a). For D distinct source specifications, it is defined as follows:

$$Q(d, x_d) = (Q^1(d, x_d), \cdots, Q^m(d, x_d)), \; x_d \in X_d \qquad (4.17)$$

$$\begin{aligned} Q^i(d, x_d) &= \alpha_d (f_5^i \circ f_4^i \circ g_3 \circ g_2 \circ p_d)(x_d) + q_d(x_d) \\ &= \alpha_d \cdot f_5^i(f_4^i(g_3(g_2(p_d(x_d))))) + q_d(x_d) \end{aligned} \qquad (4.18)$$

$$(1 \leq d \leq D, \; x_d \in X_d, \; 1 \leq i \leq m, \; \alpha_d \in \mathbb{R})$$

where q_d represents an auxiliary function for specification d (shown as the light purple sub-network on the top for Specification 1 and the light orange sub-network at the bottom for Specification D). These auxiliary functions are expected to capture the application-specific knowledge in a stronger sense than p_d functions and to separate it from the shared sub-network (shown in the dotted box). The aggregation function r_d in Fig. 4.7(a) is realized in this neural network model with a learnable parameter α_d that determines the ratio of the contribution of the shared function to the final predicted $\widetilde{QoR}$.

After the pre-training using multiple source specifications, only the shared sub-network $f_5^i \circ f_4^i \circ g_3 \circ g_2$ is transferred to a new model for the target specification. This new model also has its application-specific auxiliary part q_t, in addition to its feature function h and aggregation function r_t, that will be freshly trained for the target specification while the transferred sub-network parameters are fixed.

4.5 Experimental Results

To evaluate the performance of the presented models, a set of comprehensive DSE results is exploited from the Spector benchmark suite repository [148] containing the nine applications reported in Table 4.1. The authors of the benchmark suite synthesized the specifications using the Altera OpenCL SDK v14.1, and executed successfully synthesized designs on a Terasic DE5 board with a Stratix V FPGA. The QoR metrics of interest are the latency and utilization of the four types of resources: logic, RAM, on-chip memory, and DSP. For each of `bfs` and `spmv`, there are two sets of QoR obtained with different input datasets. The following predictive models are evaluated:

- *Single-Task Single-Domain Learning*: Model F^i in Fig. 4.3(b) for $i = 1, \cdots, 5$. Each F^i has four hidden layers with 25 nodes per hidden-layer.

- *Multi-Task Single-Domain Learning*: Model G in Fig. 4.4(c) with four hidden layers. Each hidden layer contains 125 nodes.

- *Multi-Domain Transfer Learning*: Model P in Fig. 4.6(c) for the pre-training in the source domains, and model H in 4.6(d) for the transfer learning in the target domain. Model P has one domain-specific hidden layer with ten nodes per domain, and three shared hidden layers with 125 nodes each. Model H consists of one domain-specific hidden layer with ten nodes, and the transferred sub-network from P.

- *Mixed-Sharing Multi-Domain Transfer Learning*: Mixed sharing multi-domain model Q in Fig. 4.8 for the pre-training, and a target model S as in Fig. 4.7(b) for transfer learning. Q has one domain-specific hidden layer containing ten nodes, one shared sub-network with three hidden layers each containing 100 nodes, and a domain-specific auxiliary network that has four hidden layers with 25 nodes per hidden-layer for each source domain.

The structure of the single-task model was determined empirically based on the observation that as the numbers of layers and nodes increase, the model's prediction accuracy first increases and then decreases; the structure with the peak accuracy was selected. Other models were defined to have the same number of hidden layers and nodes with the single-task

Table 4.1: Design spaces of the nine applications in the Spector dataset. Each of **bfs** and **spmv** has two versions of the QoR results.

Application	bfs_dense	bfs_sparse	dct	fir	hist	mergesort
Number of knobs	6	6	9	8	7	7
Size of design space	507	507	211	1173	896	1532

Application	mm	normals	sobel	spmv_5000	spmv_500000
Number of knobs	9	7	8	4	4
Size of design space	1180	696	1381	740	740

ones. For two transfer learning models, all applications except the target one were used as the source applications. The models were trained using the PyTorch library with the iterations of 100,000 and the learning rate of 0.001 for P and Q, and of 0.01 for all other neural networks. For each application, pre-training with P or Q took between 100 and 160 minutes using Intel i7-6700K CPU running Ubuntu 16.04.6 LTS. Training the target predictive models took between ten and 30 minutes, depending on the sample complexity. Fig. 4.9 shows the geometric mean of the *RMSE (root mean squared error)* of the four predictive models across all target applications for each of the sample size $1\%, 2\%, \cdots, 10\%$ of the design space [162]. Those RMSE values were computed after normalizing the entire DSE results X, whereas for training, *Train* sets were independently normalized. With small sample complexity from 1% to 3%, the multi-task single-domain model (marked by black asterisks) achieves lower error rates, and thus higher accuracy, than the single-task model (marked by brown circles). Transfer learning without mixed-sharing (marked by blue triangles) results in even higher error rates than the traditional single-task and multi-task learning. For all sample complexities tested, the proposed mixed-sharing multi-domain transfer learning model (marked by red squares) achieves the lowest error rates, and thus, the highest prediction accuracy.

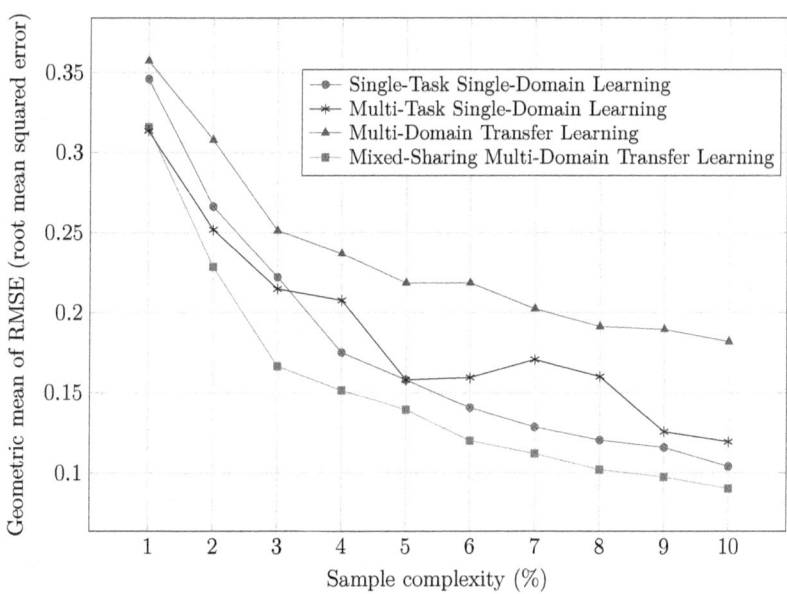

Figure 4.9: Geometric mean of RMSE across the 11 sets of HLS QoR, achieved by each of the four predictive models.

I simulated AI-augmented DSE using the Spector dataset by reading the reported QoR values instead of running HLS flows to train and test the single-task single-domain, multi-task single-domain, and mixed-sharing multi-domain transfer learning models. The two objectives of DSE in this evaluation are to minimize the latency and logic utilization; it is possible to perform a multi-dimensional DSE with more metrics. The target models were trained with 3% of the design space of each application. Then, 3% Pareto-optimal and near-optimal configurations were selected from the design space based on the predicted QoR. Fig. 4.10 shows the *ADRS (average distance from reference set)* of the proposed configurations by each model with respect to the golden Pareto-optimal set [22]. The mixed-sharing multi-domain transfer learning model achieves the lowest ADRS for most of the applications. Table 4.2 summarizes this set of experiments by presenting the geometric mean of the ADRS, achieved by each approach, across all applications. The proposed mixed-sharing multi-domain transfer

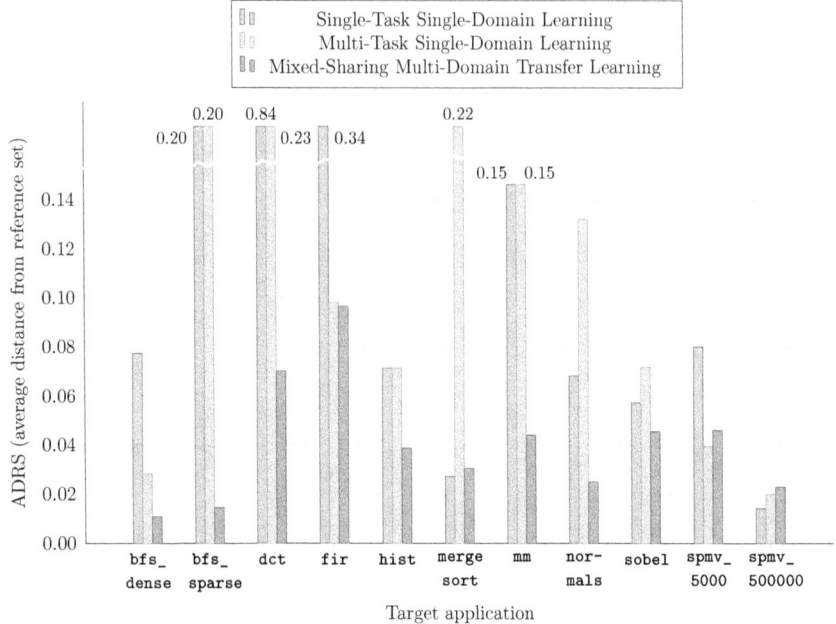

Figure 4.10: Simulated AI-augmented DSE results for the nine Spector applications with 3%-sample and 3%-proposed configurations. Each of **bfs** and **spmv** has two versions of the input.

learning model achieves the lowest mean of distances, which is equal to 0.034.

4.6 Concluding Remarks

HLS flows expedite the design of computer systems for hardware engineers, and facilitate the FPGA acceleration of applications for software engineers. To the best of my knowledge, this is the first transfer learning approach for HLS-driven DSE, where different specifications have different lists of knobs. When DSE results from other source specifications are available, successfully trained predictive models can approximate QoR without invoking HLS tools for an exhaustive DSE. As demonstrated using the Spector dataset, the proposed mixed-sharing multi-domain transfer learning model outperforms traditional machine learning models and

Table 4.2: Geometric mean of ADRS from the simulated AI-augmented DSE using the three predictive models, across the nine Spector applications with 3%-sample and 3% proposed configurations.

Predictive model	Single-task single-domain	Multi-task single-domain	Mixed-sharing multi-domain transfer learning (proposed)
Mean of ADRS	0.094	0.087	0.034

conventional transfer learning models in QoR prediction and in the simulated AI-augmented DSE. The proposed approach can enhance DSE at early stages and enable efficient DSE especially for specifications with huge design spaces.

The models presented in this chapter only consider the knob configuration spaces (as the input domains) and the QoR spaces (as the output spaces) and applies transfer learning. Ferretti et al. propose another approach that considers the application specifications, in addition to the two aforementioned spaces. For a new target application, they select the most similar application from the database of prior DSE results, and apply domain knowledge to transform Pareto-optimal configurations for the source application into configurations for the target application [165]. For both approaches, it is crucial to have access to the prior DSE results [148, 166].

The next chapter reviews and categorizes machine-learning-based approaches for the design parameter tuning problems, with CAD tools ranging from high-level synthesis to physical design.

Chapter 5: A Survey on Online and Offline Machine Learning for Design Space Exploration

Over the past decade, machine-learning-based approaches have been proposed for design space exploration of computer systems and circuits with a variety of CAD tools and flows that include high-level synthesis, logic synthesis, and physical design. They aim at finding optimal or near-optimal implementations in reduced time and cost by learning from the experience with the tools and flows. In this chapter, I review those approaches and classify them into the *online* and *offline* approaches, and into the *inside* and *outside* approaches, depending on *when* and *where* the machine learning process takes place.

5.1 Classification categories

Online algorithms receive the input incrementally and generate output in response to each input portion, whereas offline algorithms know the entire input sequence in advance [167]. When it comes to machine learning, online learners learn incrementally as new data arrives, whereas offline learners learn from past experience or data [168]. It sounds as if offline algorithms know the future and offline learners know the past, but that may be relative to when the present is. In all cases, the online counterparts do not know or process such information. It has been suggested that 'the origin of the words "on-line" and "off-line" lies in cryptographic systems, in which decryption was either done as part of the communications system (i.e., on the communication line) or after the fact by using other facilities (i.e., off the communication line)' [169]. In this regard, the machine learning approaches for design space exploration of computer systems can be categorized into online and offline approaches as follows.

Online approaches refer to the machine-learning-based approaches for design space exploration where the main learning or training is performed after a new input specification is given. Hence, the learning is done as part of the design space exploration. For those approaches, the machine learning model, agent, engine, or system is initialized for each target computer system separately because an identical CAD tool parameter or flow configuration often has diverse impacts on different specifications. *Offline approaches* are those where the main learning or training is performed using prior results before a new input specification is given. Those approaches attempt to leverage prior experience on designing different computer systems for design space exploration of a new system. Usually the main predictive model is trained offline using a large amount of prior data, and it may be briefly trained online to adapt to the new system.

Furthermore, the machine-learning-based approaches can be characterized by the target problems that they address. Most stages of CAD involve solving many intractable problems for which there exists no efficient algorithm, especially for complex specifications [170]. To address those problems, the CAD tools have employed approximate and heuristic methods, and more recently, machine learning approaches [17, 28]. Such machine learning approaches performed within the execution of CAD tools are referred to as *Inside approaches*. Those approaches improve the performance of target CAD tools and flows in general. On the other hand, the designers need to specifically determine the optimal configurations of CAD tool parameters and flow settings for each of their individual computer systems. The machine learning approaches that address this search problem that is external to CAD tools and flows are referred to as *Outside approaches*.

The following sections review a variety of machine-learning-based approaches for design space exploration with CAD tools and flows described in Chapter 2. The approaches are classified according to the aforementioned categories, as summarized in Tables 5.1, 5.2, and 5.3.

Table 5.1: Categorization of approaches: (1) Machine learning (ML) inside CAD tools.

		CAD tools		
		HLS	LS	PD
ML Approaches	Online	Reinforcement learning [171]	Multi-armed bandit [172]	Reinforcement learning [173]
	Offline	Reinforcement learning [174]	Neural networks [175]	

Table 5.2: Categorization of approaches: (2) Machine learning (ML) outside CAD tools.

		CAD tools		
		HLS	LS	PD
ML Approaches	Online	Random forest, Active learning [153], Active non-Pareto elimination [154]	Reinforcement learning [25]	Multi-armed bandit [176], Graph neural networks [177]
	Offline	Meta-heuristic [178], Transfer learning [48] (Ch. 4)	Transfer learning [179]	Reinforcement learning [180], [181]

5.2 Approaches for High-Level Synthesis

5.2.1 Online Inside approaches for HLS

As HLS transforms a high-level description into an RTL one, the first step in most HLS tools is the compilation of the input description. Haj-Ali et al. propose a reinforcement learning approach to optimize the sequence of compiler optimization phases applied to the input description [171]. To address this phase ordering problem, which is an NP-hard problem, Haj-Ali et al. first train random forests offline to determine important features of descriptions (e.g., number of branches). Then, for a specific input description, a reinforcement learning agent repeatedly selects the next optimization pass to apply, knowing the values of the important features and the history of optimization passes applied so far. This agent is

Table 5.3: Categorization of approaches: (3) Machine learning (ML) outside CAD flows.

		CAD flows			
		LSPD flows		FPGA flows	
ML	Online	Decision engine [26, 182], Bayesian optimization [184]	Multi-stage tuning [183],	Multi-armed bandit [128]	Principal component analysis,
	Offline	Recommender systems [46] (Ch. 3), Transfer learning [185]	Hybrid approach [49] (Ch. 6)	Model stacking [186]	Bayesian [130]

trained with the goal of maximizing the total rewards that are defined as the numbers of cycle counts reduced by taking each action.

5.2.2 Offline Inside approaches for HLS

Chen et al. propose a reinforcement learning approach for one of the most critical stages in HLS: scheduling [174]. Given a data flow graph whose nodes represent operations and edges represent data dependency, a schedule is a mapping of each node to a control step, satisfying the dependency relation. The objective of the time-constrained scheduling problem is to find a schedule that minimizes the number of the resources (e.g., the number of the same type of operations at the same control step). An ASAP (as soon as possible) schedule maps each node to the earliest possible control step. The reinforcement learning agent starts from an ASAP schedule, and takes a sequence of actions of moving one operation in the schedule to the next control step. The agent attempts to find an optimal policy to maximize the total rewards that are defined as the amounts of the resources reduced by taking each action. A deep neural network that represents the policy is trained once with a large amount of generated graphs, and used for scheduling new graphs.

Both Haj-Ali et al. [171] and Chen et al. [174] apply reinforcement learning to address problems within HLS. While both approaches have a mixture of offline and online properties, the former is classified as an Online approach because the main learning part is performed after a new input description is given[1], whereas it is performed using a generated dataset in the latter, which is classified as an Offline approach. In the rest of this chapter as well, the approaches are classified as Online or Offline depending on when the main learning or training occurs[2].

5.2.3 Online Outside approaches for HLS

The two main inputs to an HLS tool are the high-level specification and a configuration of the tool parameters. Online Outside approaches attempt to generate optimal configurations for each input specification. Liu et al. perform active learning via Transductive Experimental Design to sample representative and hard-to-predict configurations [153]. The HLS tool is repeatedly executed with the sampled configurations whose results are fed to train a random forest for predicting the area and latency. Meng et al. also actively sample configurations to run the HLS tool and use them to train random forests, but instead of improving the prediction accuracy, they iteratively eliminate non-Pareto optimal implementations from the candidates [154].

5.2.4 Offline Outside approaches for HLS

Offline Outside approaches exploit the CAD results of previous computer systems to train a model that can be applied online for a new system. Wang et al. train predictive models for tuning hyper-parameters of the meta-heuristic methods (e.g., the simulated annealing, genetic algorithm, and ant colony optimization) for design space exploration with HLS [178]. The predictive models are trained offline, and exploited online to tune the hyper-parameters of the meta-heuristics for new systems.

Chapter 4 of this **book** addresses another Offline Outside approach for HLS. The

---

[1] The authors also demonstrate the potential to generalize a trained policy to process new input descriptions. The generalization version would belong to the offline approaches.

[2] The distinction may be subtle in some cases. The purpose of this classification is not to disregard certain aspects of the proposed approaches but to focus on and emphasize their major contributions.

proposed approach performs transfer learning, which aims to improve the performance of a target task by reusing the knowledge extracted from different but related source tasks [48]. The knowledge extraction is usually executed offline, whereas the target task may be executed online. In the context of design space exploration, the source tasks are related to the tuning problem for prior computer systems, and the target task is defined for a new system. This approach trains an input-dependent neural network model on prior data and transfers only the input-independent part to a new model for new systems.

5.3 Approaches for Logic Synthesis

5.3.1 Online Inside approaches for LS

Yu proposes an approach that addresses an important problem within the LS stage: Boolean logic optimization [172]. Given a Boolean circuit in the form of a directed acyclic graph (where the nodes represent logic gates and the edges represent wires), the optimization is performed by applying a sequence of synthesis transformations to the graph. Yu proposes a multi-armed bandit approach, which is a class of reinforcement learning, that chooses a sequence of strategies (synthesis transformations) from a set of multiple strategies with the goal of maximizing the total payoff (e.g., the reduced number of AND-Inverter graphs).

5.3.2 Offline Inside approaches for LS

Neto et al. propose a framework for addressing a subtask of LS [175]. The proposed framework partitions the input circuit into smaller pieces and uses an artificial neural network to classify them into the two categories of representation: the And-Inverter Graph (AIG), and the Majority-Inverter Graph (MIG). The AIG partitions are likely to be optimized well with AIG optimizers, whereas the MIG partitions may prefer MIG optimizers, for the logic optimization step during LS. The classification neural network is trained offline using a generated dataset.

5.3.3 Online Outside approaches for LS

Hosny et al. define an LS tool configuration as a permutation with repetition of several primitive transformations and propose a reinforcement learning approach to obtain a configuration with a minimized area subject to a timing constraint [25]. Over the state space defined with the representative characteristics of the output gate-level description, the reinforcement learning agent performs actions of adding a primitive transformation to the configuration, with the goal of maximizing the reward that increases when the area decreases. The LS tool is repeatedly initialized and executed over many episodes of the training.

5.3.4 Offline Outside approaches for LS

Yu et al. propose a transfer learning approach for LS [179]. They use a Long Short-Term Memories network, which is a class of recurrent neural network, for predicting QoR (e.g., the critical path delay) from an LS parameter configuration (a list of applied synthesis transformations at each time frame). The neural network model is trained offline using a generated dataset, and updated online for a new computer system and manufacturing process technology.

5.4 Approaches for Physical Design

5.4.1 Online Inside approaches for PD

Elgammal et al. propose a reinforcement learning approach for the placement stage in PD for FPGAs [173]. The reinforcement learning agent interacts with a simulated-annealing-based placer that applies a sequence of moves (changing the location of some netlist blocks) to an initial solution. The agent repeatedly proposes a candidate move to apply in order to maximize the reward defined as the reduction in the normalized placement cost.

5.4.2 Online Outside approaches for PD

Stefanidis et al. propose a multi-armed bandit approach to repeatedly select the next heuristic algorithm to apply, among the three gate-sizing heuristics and among the four buffering heuristics. The gate-sizing and buffering interleave [176]. Given a netlist after floorplanning, Lu et al. performs cell clustering via unsupervised learning. The resulting clusters are fed into the placement tool [177]. Both approaches are considered as Outside approaches because the addressed problems have been conventionally solved by the designers. As CAD tools continue to advance, future versions of PD tools may address such problems. In that case, the above approaches would be classified as Inside approaches.

5.4.3 Offline Outside approaches for PD

Mirhoseini et al. propose a reinforcement learning approach for the chip floorplanning step in the placement stage of PD [180]. Their approach focuses on generalizing the problem so that a reinforcement learning policy network trained with a large set of previous computer systems can effectively guide the placement of a new system. For this, they first train a graph neural network that embeds the netlist information and predicts the reward defined as a linear combination of the approximate wirelength, congestion, and density. This neural network (except the last prediction layer) is used as the encoder of the reinforcement learning policy network. The trained policy network may also be fine-tuned online for new systems.

Agnesina et al. propose another reinforcement learning approach for tuning the placement parameters to minimize the wirelength [181]. Given the state defined by the netlist information and the current placement parameter settings, the reinforcement learning agent performs an action of modifying the parameter settings (e.g., flip Boolean parameter values, or increase integer parameter values). The netlist information includes the handcrafted features (e.g., the number of cells, and floorplan area) and the extracted features using a graph neural network. After the agent is trained on a set of computer systems, it can operate for new systems using the learned policy.

5.5 Approaches for Logic Synthesis and Physical Design flows

5.5.1 Online Outside approaches for LSPD

Ziegler et al. propose a Bayesian-inspired decision engine for tuning extremely large-sacle LSPD (logic synthesis and physical design) flows for designing industrial high-performance computer systems [26, 182]. The online decision engine incrementally and adaptively constructs parameter configurations to run the LSPD flows with. Ma et al. perform an explicit Bayesian optimization in the LSPD flow tuning to minimize the QoR values [184]. In each iteration, an acquisition function samples a configuration, and the LSPD flow is executed with that configuration to output the QoR values, which are used to update a surrogate model. Given a configuration, the surrogate model based on Gaussian process regression outputs a predicted QoR value (a single QoR value or a weighted sum of multiple QoR values) along with the uncertainty of the prediction. The acquisition function exploits the updated surrogate model to sample a new configuration in the next iteration.

5.5.2 Offline Outside approaches for LSPD

Chapter 3 of this book addresses an Offline Outside approach for LSPD flows [46]. The proposed approach performs customized recommendation, motivated by a movie recommender system that learns the relationship between movies and users from many different users ratings on various movies and makes a personalized recommendation to the users. This approach trains a QoR prediction model on a collection of prior data and makes a customized recommendation for each computer system. The prediction model is trained offline, whereas the recommended parameter configurations are built online for new systems. Davis et al. propose a transfer learning approach for QoR prediction in RTL-to-GDS flows [185]. A neural network model is trained offline for predicting the QoR values from the flow parameters using a prior dataset. For new systems, only the last layers of the trained model are re-trained online with a small number of the CAD flow runs.

5.5.3 Hybrid Outside approaches for LSPD

While the main machine learning part is executed offline, many of the *Offline* approaches discussed above include an online adaptation part for new computer systems. The fundamental difference between those online adaptation parts and the *Online* approaches is that the former requires a trained model or obtained knowledge from the offline learning part whereas the latter can be performed without any prior data. The *Online-Offline Hybrid* approaches consist of both online and offline machine learning parts such that the online learning can be carried out immediately without prior data or models. Liang et al. propose a multi-stage approach that consists of the online parameter tuning and the offline warm-up [183]. For each stage of an LSPD flow (e.g., LS, placement, CTS, routing, and optimizations), an ant-colony optimization engine suggests the settings of the parameters for that individual stage, while cooperating across all stages to evaluate the settings (by running the LSPD flows). This online flow tuning may be enhanced via the offline warm-up that initializes the online engines and reduces the number of parameters to be tuned by grouping the frequently interacting ones and selecting only the important ones determined from the archived data. Chapter 6 of this book proposes another hybrid approach for LSPD flows in [49]. The proposed system includes both online and offline subsystems such that the online system evaluates, combines, and refines the parameter settings while the offline system may provide recommended settings using prediction models trained on the archived data.

5.6 Approaches for FPGA flows

5.6.1 Online Outside approaches for FPGAs

Xu et al. propose a parallel multi-armed bandit approach for tuning the parameters of an FPGA compilation flow (from an RTL description to a configuration bitstream) [128]. The search space defined by the (discretized) FPGA parameters grows exponentially with respect to the number of parameters; hence, the proposed approach dynamically partitions the search space into subspaces to be explored in parallel on multiple machines. The partitions are made without any prior knowledge and based on the information gains, measured after the initial FPGA flow runs with a number of sample parameter settings for the input specification. Then, they exploit a multi-armed bandit method to allocate more computing resources (for running the OpenTuner, an open-source autotuning framework [187], that invokes the FPGA flows) to more promising subspaces.

5.6.2 Offline Outside approaches for FPGAs

Agnesina et al. propose an approach for tuning the parameters of an FPGA place & route flow for FPGA-based logic emulation [186]. For hard-to-compile netlists, they first train multiple base models (a random forest, extra trees, gradient-boosted trees, and an artificial neural network) that each takes in the extracted features of the input netlist and predicts the winning probability for each FPGA flow scenario. In this problem, a scenario wins if it achieves the shortest FPGA compilation time. Then, they train a stacker (a logistic regressor) that collects the output of the base models and makes a final prediction. The models are trained using a large-scale commercial FPGA compilation database.

5.6.3 Hybrid Outside approaches for FPGAs

Kapre et al. propose an online-offline hybrid approach such that the online learning can be carried out immediately without prior data or models [130]. For the goal of accelerating timing closure, the online Bayesian learning component learns to predict the total negative slack of the implementation from the settings of the (Boolean) FPGA flow parameters. The offline component performs Principal Component Analysis to reduce the number of the parameters to be tuned in order to improve the online machine learning performance.

5.7 Concluding Remarks

With the recent rise of AI, machine learning approaches have been actively proposed for AI-augmented DSE of computer systems with various CAD tools and flows. This chapter has provided an overview of the state-of-the-art machine learning approaches spanning the CAD stages of HLS, LS, and, PD, and the CAD flows of LSPD and FPGAs. Among the presented categories, the main focus of this **book** has been the Offline Outside approaches because (1) from the perspective of the user of advanced CAD tools and flows, the machine learning system exists outside the tools or flows, and (2) to address the machine learning challenges introduced in Chapter 1, it is inevitable to learn from the experience with the design and optimization of *other* computer systems.

The next chapter presents future work and concluding remarks for this **book**.

Chapter 6: Future Work and Concluding Remarks

Chapter 3 and Chapter 4 discussed AI-augmented design space exploration of computer systems with HLS tools, and with LSPD flows. Chapter 5 classified related machine learning approaches into categories of online learning and offline learning. This chapter presents future work motivated by the previous chapters and concludes the **book**.

6.1 AI-Augmented DSE with End-to-End CAD

Machine-learning-based approaches have been introduced for DSE at different steps of CAD flows. Running an entire end-to-end (E2E) flow with aggressive performance and energy efficiency goals may require different DSE techniques, e.g., one for high-level synthesis and another for logic synthesis and physical design. Moreover, along the CAD tool-chain, the decisions made at an earlier step can often both guide and constrain the pool of feasible implementations at latter steps. To address these challenges, I propose an AI-augmented DSE approach with E2E CAD flows, as shown in Fig. 6.1.

The proposed work addresses the problem of configuring many CAD tool parameters across HLS, LS, and PD by exploiting machine-learning-based approaches to configure the hyperparameters that guide the configuration of individual CAD parameters. This approach includes the development of the following three main modules.

1. Meta-optimization framework for E2E design hyperparameter configuration: A hyperparameter and CAD parameter configuration framework will flexibly support different E2E design flows, which may include specific CAD tools with tunable parameters. For instance, an individual E2E flow may consist of a sequence of specialized CAD tools and execution scripts. As illustrated in Fig. 6.1, this meta-optimization framework

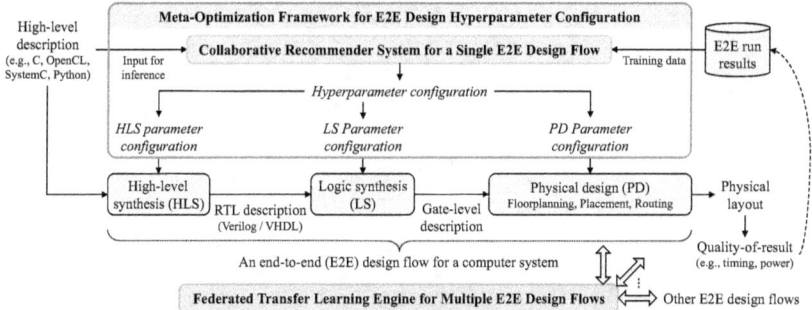

Figure 6.1: An overview of the proposed AI-augmented DSE with end-to-end CAD flows.

configures hyperparameters and passes specific parameter configurations to the CAD tools within the flow. This framework provides an environment for developing and deploying the next modules.

2. Collaborative recommender system for a single E2E design flow: A learning-based recommender system for E2E hyperparameters will leverage collaborative filtering in order to predict the final QoR for a computer system specification based on the previous results for other systems. As shown in Fig. 6.1, this recommender system is trained using a collection of E2E QoR values, and a new specification is taken as input for the inference using the trained recommender system. This recommender system approach differs from the one presented in Chapter 3 in that it also processes the specification as an input, whereas the recommender system in Chapter 3 processes only the configurations and CAD results. The recommender system becomes a building block for the next module.

3. Federated transfer learning engine for multiple E2E design flows: A federated transfer learning engine will convert trained prediction or recommendation models for other E2E design flows into an informative model for the target flow. As noted at the bottom of Fig. 6.1, this transfer learning engine interacts with multiple E2E design flows or

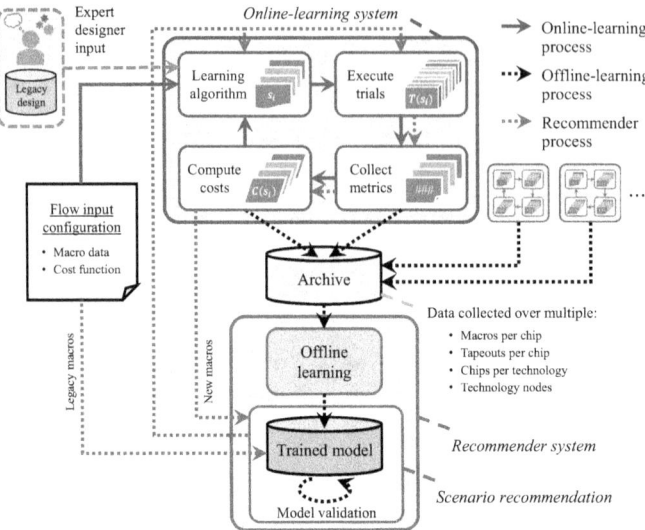

Figure 6.2: An overview of the proposed system with the interplay of online and offline machine learning [49].

a collection of E2E QoR values from those flows. This transfer learning approach performs federated learning, i.e., it trains transferable models from multiple flows where the training data are not shared across different flows. This approach would allow protecting the confidential information, an issue not explicitly addressed in Chapter 4.

6.2 Interplay of Online and Offline Machine Learning

As classified in Chapter 6, machine-learning-based approaches have been also introduced both for (1) online problems, without previous DSE experiences, and for (2) offline problems, where DSE results from other computer systems are available. For a new target computer system, the online approaches can be applied even when previous results are not available, whereas the offline approaches may enhance the performance of DSE by extracting and exploiting hidden knowledge and information from the previous results. To take advantage of both approaches depending on the design environment and data availability, I (with M.

Ziegler and L. Carloni) propose a hybrid approach where the online and offline components interplay and interact with each other. Fig. 6.2 illustrates an overview of the proposed hybrid system.

The proposed system consists of three main components: (1) an online-learning system, (2) a data archive, and (3) a recommender system. The aim of the overall system is to create a holistic approach that can cover all phases of the design cycle and availability of suitable training data set. For example, if little or no suitable training data is available, the system can emphasize the online-learning system. However, as the data archive contains suitable training data, the system can utilize the recommender system. The system also inherently supports hybrid or mixed-mode online and offline approaches. For example, the scenarios originating from the recommender system can be mixed with scenarios from the online component and iteratively refined. Furthermore, the system can take scenarios from additional source of prior knowledge. For example, in an industrial setting, there are often legacy designs that could provide useful scenarios that would be beneficial to the iterative refinement process. The legacy design scenarios may not exist in the data archive, as they could be generated using ad hoc methods. Expert designers can also directly supply input to the online system.

6.3 Concluding Remarks

To address the challenges of increased design complexity, high-performance goals, power constraints, time-to-market pressures, and non-recurring engineering cost, CAD approaches have evolved towards raising the level of abstraction in the design process. Along this path of evolution, DSE problems have progressed to work with the corresponding level of abstraction. Designers not only specify the computer system at a high level of abstraction, but also control the compute-intensive HLS, LS, and PD flow by configuring the corresponding CAD tool options and flow settings. For each of those problems, DSE approaches have advanced towards exploiting a variety of optimization algorithms and techniques. Over the past decade, machine-learning-based methods have been proposed as state-of-the-art approaches for DSE problems at all major levels of abstraction. This book has proposed novel machine-learning-based approaches that learn from past experience with different computer systems to augment the DSE of new systems.

Heterogeneity has emerged as a key to resolving the fundamental trade-off between high performance and low power dissipation of computer systems. Designers design each of the various heterogeneous subsystems of computer systems and specialized accelerators. To cope with, and even to leverage, the increased degree of heterogeneity and number of distinct subsystems, this book has investigated the potential to effectively and efficiently learn from the DSE experience with different systems and subsystems. One of the main takeaways is not only to find common properties among computer systems and apply similar param-eter configurations, but to grasp the underlying relationship among heterogeneous systems and their reactions to the CAD tools and flows in order to generate customized parameter configurations.

Both the level of design abstraction and the degree of heterogeneity may continue to increase over time. Domain-specific design languages allow designers to specify a domain-specific hardware accelerator with a much smaller number of lines of code than for HLS [188]. Emerging devices and technology, such as quantum computing [189], nuromorphic computing [190], optical computing [191, 192], and optical communications [193], prompt the need for developing or modifying CAD tools and flows accordingly. In such cases, AI-augmented DSE approaches will face another challenge; nevertheless, they are expected to enhance the design process to a greater degree when it is possible to learn from the diverse experience.